David Sanger

PLAY THE ORGAN

Volume Two

Order No: NOV 01 0235

NOVELLO PUBLISHING LIMITED

To all my students, past and present

Cover design by Roland Piper

ISBN: 0-85360-153-4
Order No: NOV 01 0235

CONTENTS

Foreword

The first volume of *Play the Organ* was the official tutor of National Learn the Organ Year 1990. The publication of this second volume coincides with the first anniversary of the follow-on project, the National Organ Teachers' Encouragement Scheme (NOTES), and so it is fitting that this volume is likewise endorsed.

Under NLOY nearly two thousand people, young and old, registered as beginner or re-starter organists. The very success of the year exposed a serious shortage of organ teachers and so NOTES was formed to tackle this problem by encouraging more people, especially younger organists, to consider teaching as an essential part of their career. NOTES also exists to promote good organ teaching which takes account of the changes in the organ world mentioned in the foreword to volume 1. A national register of organ teachers, distributed by The Royal College of Organists, has been compiled.

The art of teaching the organ, as with teaching in general, represents an interaction between teacher and pupil (already, much of NOTES' work has been of benefit to both groups) and it is with this in mind that we welcome the appearance of the second volume of *Play the Organ.*

the NOTES committee

DAVID SANGER is an organ recitalist of international repute, having toured in many countries and recorded many CDs covering a wide ranging repertoire. He has long experience as a private teacher of organ and has given many Master Classes at home and abroad. He has been a Professor at The Royal Academy of Music for some years, culminating in his being Head of the Organ Department for two years, and, since moving to Cumbria, he has remained on the staff there as a Consultant Professor. He also teaches many organ scholars at the Universities of Oxford and Cambridge. Several of his organ students have been successful at national and international competition.

Preface

Play the Organ – A Beginner's Tutor (Novello & Co., 1990) was written in conjunction with National Learn the Organ Year, 1990, to encourage students to learn to play the pipe-organ, even if they had no previous keyboard experience.

Play the Organ Volume Two is not only intended for players who have completed the Beginner's Tutor, but also for those with a knowledge and some mastery of keyboard technique (Grade 4 piano of the Associated Board of the Royal Schools of Music, or equivalent).

It is inevitable that there will be some duplication of material for the student who has completed the Beginner's Tutor, but those sections already covered may be ignored, or treated as an opportunity for revision.

The intending organ student is strongly advised to seek the guidance of a qualified teacher at an early stage; failure to do this may result in problems with technique, difficult to eradicate at a later stage.

Acknowledgements

Thanks are due to the following:
The late Dr. Peter le Huray, who kindly gave valuable information about early fingering techniques; Deborah Johnson of Trafalgar Publishing, Birmingham, for her patience in guiding me through the Novello archives; Stephen Farr, Michael Perkins and Joy Sanger for reading through the script, and for their helpful comments; Relf Clark for his help with Romantic British registration; Marie Ziener for her repertoire suggestions; J. W. Walker & Sons Ltd. for providing some of the photos, and the diagram at the end of the volume; and Leslie East, Jonathan Dore and the rest of the team at Novello for their painstaking work.

D.S.

List of works included

Chapter 1

Applicatio, BWV 994	J. S. Bach, 1685-1750
Minuet no. 17 from the *Clock Pieces*	J. Haydn, 1732-1809
2 part, manuals only:	
Allein Gott in der Höh sei Ehr, BWV 711	J. S. Bach
3 part, manuals only:	
Befiehl du deine Wege	F. W. Marpurg, 1718-95
(ed. Emery)	
4 part, manuals only:	
Kyrie, Gott Vater in Ewigkeit, BWV 672	J. S. Bach
Prelude in C, from BWV 870a	J. S. Bach
(ed. Peter le Huray)	
2 Fugues on the Magnificat	J. Pachelbel, 1653-1706
(ed. Emery)	

Chapter 2

Pedal-Exercitium BWV 598	J. S. Bach
(ending by author)	

Chapter 3

left hand and pedals:	
Exercises 1, 2 and 3 for left hand and pedals	C. H. Rinck, 1770-1846
from *Practical Organ School, Part 1*	
Exercise (123) for left hand and pedals	W. G. Alcock, 1861-1947
from *The Organ*	
simple trio-playing:	
Trio Exercise (146)	W. G. Alcock
from *The Organ*	
Chorale varied in 3 parts	Hamilton, 19th century
from *Catechism*, pub. 1850	
Variation on Liebster Jesu	C. H. Rinck
from *Practical Organ School, Part 2*	
Nun ruhen alle Wälder	Armin Knab, 1881-1951
from *Sieben Orgelchoräle*	
4 part, including pedals:	
No. 1 from *12 Studies*	Adolf Hesse, 1809-63

Prelude no. 1 in C, of 30 Preludes	C. H. Rinck
from *Practical Organ School, Part 1*	
Andante, opus 15 no. 9	Gustav Merkel,
Andante, opus 15 no. 1	1827-85
Prelude no. 2 in A minor	C. H. Rinck
Prelude no. 8 in F# minor	
from *Practical Organ School, Part 1*	
more advanced trio-playing:	
Jesu, meine Freude [part of]	F. W. Marpurg
(ed. Emery)	
[Trio] from Concerto per la Chiesa	G. P. Telemann,
arr. J. G. Walther, 1684-1748	1681-1767
(ed. Prince)	
Schmücke dich, O liebe Seele	F. W. Marpurg
(ed. Emery)	
Inventio in C	H. N. Gerber, 1702-75
Inventio in A minor	
(ed. Susi Jeans)	
Trio in F, opus 49 no. 10	J. Rheinberger,
Trio in D flat, opus 49 no. 4	1839-1901
Ertödt uns durch dein' Güte	J. S. Bach, arr. Trevor

Chapter 4

British music:	
(Verse)	Benjamin Cosyn,
(ed. Langley, from *English Organ Music*	1572-1652
series, Novello)	
A Double Voluntary	John Blow, 1649-1708
(ed. Langley, from *English Organ Music*	
series, Novello)	
(Cornet) Voluntary	John Robinson,
(ed. Susi Jeans)	1682-1762
German music:	
Echo alio modo	Samuel Scheidt,
	1587-1654
Praeludium in G minor	Franz Tunder, 1614-67
Lass mich dein sein un bleiben	Delphin Strungck,
	1600/01-94

Ornaments and accidentals in brackets, small accidentals, and slurs and ties with short vertical lines (e.g. ⌐⊤¬) are editorial. Unless otherwise indicated, exercises are by the author. Fingerings and pedallings throughout (except for BWV 870a and 994) are also by the author. All metronome markings are suggestions by the author, indicating a possible peformance pace. It is advisable to start learning each piece slowly, gradually increasing the tempo during the learning process, eventually attaining the suggested tempo.

Introduction

DESCRIPTION OF THE PIPE-ORGAN*

It is very difficult to generalize about organs, because they are all so different. They vary from a very small keyboard comprising just a few keys (known as a PORTATIVE†) to a mighty construction of several keyboards operating thousands of pipes of different shapes and sizes. If we play the average church pipe-organ with two MANUALS (keyboards played by the hands) and PEDALBOARD (played by the feet), we can discover most that we need to know about basic organ-playing technique (you might transfer to a larger instrument at a later stage). The pipe-organ is a collection of different families of wind-blown instruments, and if properly sited in a church or hall can easily fill the building with enough sound to support large numbers of people singing strongly. Its splendid repertoire, spanning several centuries, is large and varied, and sufficient to employ the serious organist with a life-time's study.

The organ has a long tradition in many countries and it is mostly associated with the church. The instrument generally accepted as the oldest organ in the world can still be heard to this day at St Valeria, Sion (Sitton) in Switzerland, and it possibly dates from 1380!

Many changes have taken place in the style and building of organs over the centuries, especially since the advent of electricity. But more recently, organ-building has taken what could be described as an 'about turn' with the Organ Reform Movement, returning to basic principles and disciplines. In many organs of recent years electricity is used only to power the motor which drives the blower to produce the wind, but apart from that there are few changes from organs of centuries ago.

Describing the mechanics of the instrument is not easy, since the internal parts vary so much from one style of instrument to another. For example, an organ might be controlled by MECHANICAL ACTION (commonly known as TRACKER ACTION), pneumatic action, electric action or a combination of these. The ACTION is the means of contact between the keys and pipes, and it is fairly important that the instrument on which you

*Those who have worked through Volume 1 may treat the Introduction as revision, or move on to Chapter 1.

†All words in SMALL CAPITALS are defined in the Glossary.

Photo reproduced from 'The Organ' by William Sumner by permission of Macdonald & Co.

The Sion organ, c. 1380 (the pedal pipes at the back were added in the 18th century).

decide to learn has a good responsive ACTION, preferably MECHANICAL. It is not the purpose of this Tutor to enter into great detail about the mechanical or electrical workings of the organ. These are covered in other books. There is, however, a diagram at the end of the Tutor showing the layout of a traditional organ, and a reading list containing some helpful books on the topic.

FINDING A PIPE-ORGAN ON WHICH TO LEARN

Try to gain access to the instrument in your local church, and see if it is an average two- (or three-) MANUAL and PEDAL pipe-organ (the PEDALBOARD should have at least 30 'black and white' notes, and the MANUALS at least 56 each). If so, and if you request politely, you may be given some practice-time in which you can discover aspects of the instrument for yourself. Sometimes a small charge is made for practising. (When practising in the winter months, extra warm clothing should be worn!) It is possible to learn at a larger instrument, but at a small organ (such as a single-manual or one without pedals) it would be hard to master certain aspects of basic technique. It is important that you discover how to switch the organ on and off, and also that you protect the security of the church by finding out how to lock up after you have had your practice session.

POSITION AT THE CONSOLE

Let's assume that you are now in the church and the instrument is at your disposal. The first thing you need to do is to seat yourself comfortably at the CONSOLE in readiness to play. (CONSOLE is the name for the piece of furniture, either attached or detached from the workings of the organ, at which you sit and play). It is inadvisable to stand on the pedal keys while you are climbing onto the stool, and at many organs it is necessary to slide along the stool from one end in order to get to the middle because of restricted space at the player's back. Sometimes a cushion or material runner may be found on the stool surface. Such comforts must be removed before starting to play, as they will severely hamper freedom of movement. For safety reasons, over-zealous church cleaners should be discouraged from polishing the top surface of an organ stool!

The height of the stool may be adjustable, but such stools are rare in British churches. If the stool is too low for comfortable pedalling, wooden blocks (or perhaps some old hymn-books) of suitable thickness may be placed under the legs of the bench to raise it to a suitable height. Unfortunately, no such easy remedy can be applied if the stool is too high!

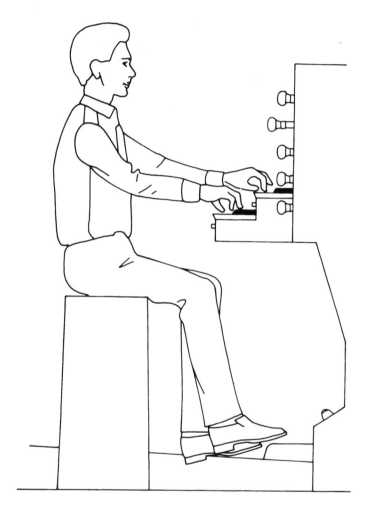

You will notice that the compass (or range) of the organ's keyboard is smaller than that of the piano. Look at this diagram and check that you are in the right position.

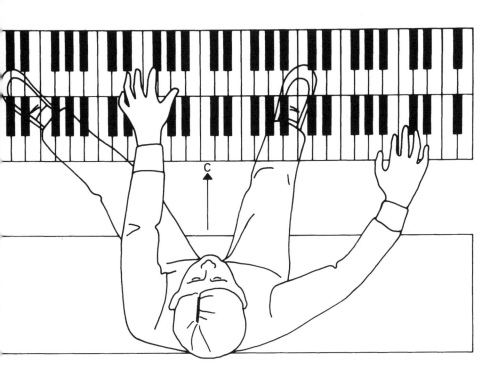

Middle **C** should be pointing roughly at your navel!

THE CONSOLE

If the organ has DRAW STOPS,

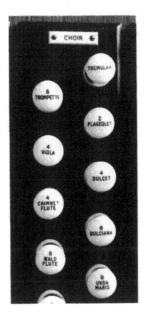

at least one of these has to be drawn for any sound to be possible. Likewise, if it has TAB STOPS,

at least one has to be switched down before any sound may be made. There are so many different names for organ STOPS that it would take another book to cover them all! However, to understand the STOPS on your practice organ, it is helpful to find out which tradition of organ-building it belongs to — it may be in the English Victorian or Romantic style, neo-Baroque or some other style. The names of the STOPS often give a clue; for example, the fundamental tone of the organ in Britain is based on the STOP called OPEN DIAPASON 8' (playable from the GREAT or lower MANUAL in a two-manual or the middle MANUAL in a three-manual organ), but since the recent influence of continental organs in this country, you will frequently find this stop called Prinzipal 8' or Montre 8'. In Chapter 4 you will find SPECIFICATIONS (i.e. STOP lists) from Britain, Germany and France, which should assist in understanding STOP names, and eventually lead to greater knowledge in the choice of STOPS.

Try to gain an understanding of the numbers usually engraved on the stopknobs. For an explanation of these see below, under **Stops and their pitches.**

Some CONSOLES have various means by which combinations of STOPS may be drawn. These are called THUMB PISTONS when they are placed immediately beneath each manual, TOE PISTONS when just above the pedalboard or COMPOSITION PEDALS when operated by a foot lever. It is not necessary at this stage to understand their function in detail.

There is often a section (or 'department') of the organ in which the pipes are enclosed in a wooden box. This is fitted with venetian-blind-type shutters and is generally called the SWELL. In a two-manual organ this is the upper of the two keyboards (hereafter called MANUALS) and a *crescendo* or *diminuendo* (i.e. gradual increase or decrease in volume) may be made by opening and closing the shutters by means of a pedal or lever.

It is important when leaving your practice instrument to remember to leave the SWELL-box open to allow circulation of air at an even temperature, thus helping to keep the tuning of the SWELL department in line with the rest of the instrument. See Chapter 7 for a photograph of two different types of SWELL pedal.

If you find your practice organ has a third MANUAL this is probably known as the CHOIR, or POSITIVE. This is always the lowest manual.

STOPS AND THEIR PITCHES

Any STOP with 8′ on its label will sound at 'piano pitch' (that is to say the pitch at which you would expect a piano to sound). In the case of the OPEN DIAPASON 8′ this means that the longest pipe played by the lowest note on the manuals will have a length of 8 feet from its mouth to the top of the pipe (this distance is known as the 'speaking length'). This pipe will often form part of the front pipe-display in the CASEWORK, situated above the player's head. It is sometimes possible to play the lowest note with the STOP drawn and hear the wind rushing into the pipe as it sounds. STOPS which are marked 4′ will sound an octave higher than this and consequently the longest of these pipes will have a speaking length of 4′, while those of 2′ pitch are an octave higher again. Likewise, 16′ STOPS will sound an octave lower than 'piano pitch', and 32′ STOPS an octave lower again. MIXTURES and COMPOUND STOPS are described later this chapter, on page 8, and MUTATION STOPS are explained in the Glossary.

Those STOPS which enable a pipe to 'speak' or sound are known as 'speaking stops'. Each speaking stop has its own row or rows of pipes known as a RANK or RANKS. As will be seen from the photographs below, pipes come in all different shapes and sizes, but in general, the same type of pipe is found throughout the range of the keyboard for each stop. The rising pitch from bass to treble is achieved by a gradual reduction in the length and circumference of the pipes. On the right is a photograph of OPEN DIAPASON pipes from the bottom of the keyboard to the top.

Some RANKS are closed or sealed at the top by a stopper, and these are known as 'stopped pipes'. A stopped pipe sounds an octave lower than an unstopped pipe, and it will produce a more 'flutey' tone. Thus, the Stopped Diapason 8′ is classed as a FLUTE STOP, and not a DIAPASON. It has pipes of half the length of its open counterpart, yet sounds at the same pitch.

The STRING-toned STOPS such as Gambas, Violas, Salicionals and Celestes, which are never stopped, have much narrower pipes than the OPEN DIAPASON, and their tone is consequently much more keen.

All the above-mentioned pipes are known as FLUE pipes, not to be confused with FLUTES which are just one type of FLUE.

The other category of pipework is known as REEDS. The REED STOPS such as Trumpets, Clarions, Cornopeans, Horns, Oboes and Clarinets, produce their characteristic tones by means of a REED, or brass tongue, found in the foot of the pipe (known as the boot). The pipes then fashion the tone produced by the REED according to the sound required.

Some different types of pipe:

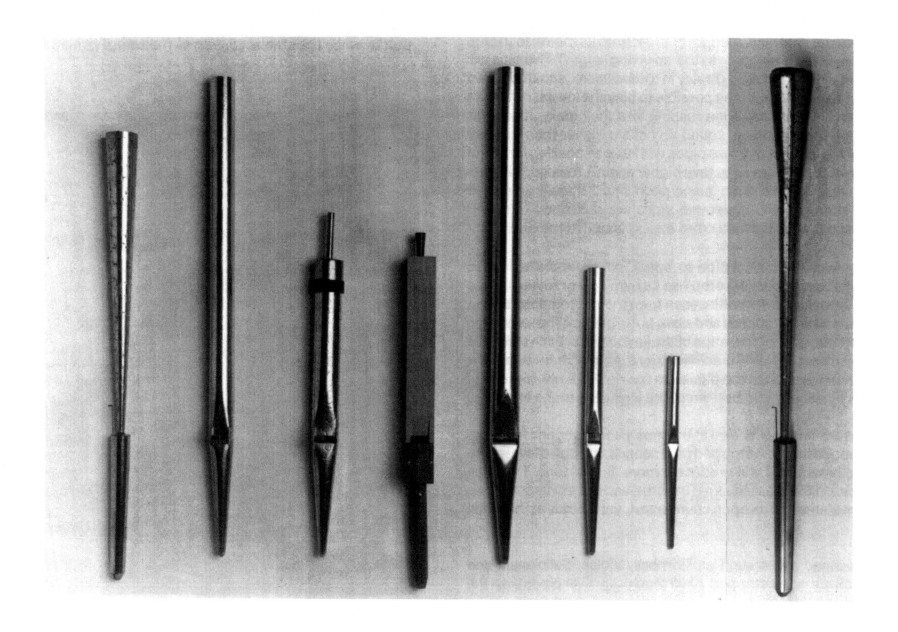

(from left to right): Trumpet, Gamba, Chimney Flute, Stopped Diapason, Open Diapason, Principal, Fifteenth and Oboe.

The organ student should learn how to select appropriate STOPS for the repertoire. Sometimes composers give detailed instructions, although not every organ has the required STOPS, and compromises have to be made. Where there are no instructions, the knowledge and taste of the organist come into play. The art of REGISTRATION is discussed in some detail later in the Tutor. It will be of great benefit to the student to seek help and advice from an experienced teacher on the matter of mixing and matching different STOPS, or families of STOPS.

As mentioned earlier, STOPS may be listed under the following headings: DIAPASONS, FLUTES, STRINGS and REEDS, and in most organs at least one STOP may be found in each category (or family). The following list of selected STOPS often found in British organs shows how they may be categorized*:

Diapasons: Double Diapason 16', Open Diapason(s) 8', Principal 4' (or Octave 4'), Twelfth 2⅔' (or Quint 2⅔'), Fifteenth 2' (or Superoctave 2'), Mixture 4 ranks (There are many names for the different types of Mixture — known as COMPOUND STOPS — e.g., Furniture, Sesquialtera, Harmonics, each with a variable number of RANKS. See p.8.)

Flutes: Bourdon 16', Stopped Diapason 8' (or Hohl Flute 8', or Wald Flute 8'), Harmonic Flute 4', Nazard 2⅔', Piccolo 2', Tierce 1⅗', Larigot 1⅓', Sifflöte 1'.

Strings: Contra Viole 16', Viola 8', Gamba 8', Salicional 8', Voix Celeste 8' (this latter stop is tuned to undulate with the Salicional or Gamba and must only be used along with one of them), Dulciana 8', Unda Maris 8', Vox Angelica 8' (these latter three STOPS are not strictly considered STRINGS. They are more appropriately categorized as very mild Diapasons. The latter two are similarly tuned to undulate with the Dulciana and must only be used along with it).

Reeds: Trombone 16' (or Posaune 16' or Ophicleide 16'), Trumpet 8' (or Cornopean 8' or Horn 8'), Clarion 4', Fagotto 16', Oboe 8'.

The Diapasons of the GREAT organ (the term 'organ' is often used for

*There are many alternative STOP names. Those given represent the most common. Stops sounding at intervals other than the unison or its octaves are known as MUTATIONS (e.g. Twelfth 2⅔', Nazard 2⅔', Tierce 1⅗', Larigot 1⅓').

each department or division within the instrument, as well as the name for the whole) are designed and VOICED to form a CHORUS, usually with only one STOP at each pitch. In building up to the full Diapason Chorus, one of these sequences is normally followed (from *mezzo piano* to *forte*):
1.   8; 8 + 4; 8 + 4 + 2; 8 + 4 + 2⅔ + 2; 8 + 4 + 2⅔ + 2 + Mixture.
2.   8; 8 + 4; 16 + 8 + 4; 16 + 8 + 4 + 2; 16 + 8 + 4 + 2⅔ + 2; 16 + 8 + 4 + 2⅔ + 2 + Mixture.

(Note that these are guidelines. Exceptions to the use of the above combinations will be found in Chapters 4 and 7).

It is inadvisable to leave gaps in the above Diapason Chorus combinations (e.g., 8 + MIXTURE) in most organs, because the CHORUS is designed as a cumulative unit.

One of the fundamental aspects of registering the organ repertoire is recognizing and understanding the CHORUS (especially the Diapason Chorus). If the organ contained stops at 8' pitch only (i.e., piano pitch), it would be at a disadvantage in supporting the voices of a congregation, as such STOPS would have to be placed on heavy wind-pressure for the sound to carry sufficiently, resulting in a rather unpleasant sound. (There are, however, many instances in large organs where selected STOPS — especially REEDS — are placed on 'heavy wind', in order to enable melodies to be 'soloed', or to create a 'fanfare' effect). Particular STOPS are, therefore, necessary to reinforce the fundamental tone, and this so-called UPPERWORK, along with the fundamental tone, forms the CHORUS, a characteristic feature of the organ.

To make this clearer, consider, for example, the structure of the sound of the lowest C of the OPEN DIAPASON 8'. The note, when played, is accompanied by a varying number of attendant pitches (in decreasing intensity) called *harmonics*, *overtones*, or *upper partials*.

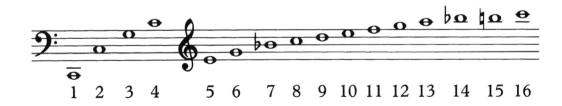

1 2 3 4   5 6   7 8 9 10 11 12 13 14 15 16

Thus the note **C** may be accompanied by (2) the octave **C** above, (3) the **G** above that (12th), (4) the **C** above that (15th), (5) the **E** above that (17th), and so on, the intervals between the notes getting smaller as the series ascends, and progressively of less intensity.

Thus the tonal characteristics of the **C** (or of any other note) may be strengthened by the addition of other stops at higher pitches. The addition of the PRINCIPAL 4' will strengthen the 2nd harmonic; the Twelfth 2⅔' will strengthen the 3rd; the Fifteenth 2', the 4th harmonic, and so on. The addition of the MIXTURE 4' ranks will strengthen four more harmonics in the series. Some MIXTURES have numbers of the STOP-knobs. These show which particular pitches are represented, and may be ascertained by counting the white-notes upwards from the low **C**; e.g., if the designation is 12.15.19.22., one would expect to find the following pitches sounding when the low **C** is depressed:

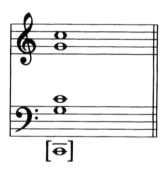

Likewise, if the designation is 17.19.22., one would expect to find the following pitches sounding when the low **C** is depressed:

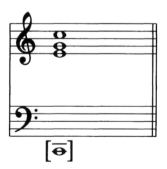

In MIXTURE STOPS, those pitches not tuned to the unison (in the above examples, the **G**s and **E**; nos. 3, 5 and 6 in the harmonic series) will be

tuned 'pure' (without beats), and correspond to the harmonic structure of the low C. Their tuning will, therefore, not be identical to the equivalent notes in the equally tempered scale. (The same applies to MUTATION STOPS).

As the RANKS of the MIXTURES ascend in pitch, and the pipes become smaller, it is often necessary for some, or all, RANKS to 'break back'; i.e., they double back to reinforce the harmonics which are within the usual human audible range, thus creating greater brilliance in the treble register.

The organ CHORUS, when properly constructed, is a well-matched series of sounds at different pitches, enhancing the fundamental tone.

The FLUTES may also form a CHORUS, although they do not have the strength of the DIAPASONS. The CORNET 5 ranks is a CHORUS of open or stopped FLUTES which is usually combined to be activated by one STOP-knob (another COMPOUND STOP). Its ranks blend together to make a homogeneous, slightly reedy tone. Each note played causes five wide-scaled FLUTE pipes to sound at the following pitches: 8', 4', 2⅔', 2' and 1⅗' (the first 5 notes in the harmonic series), and it is the 1⅗' which gives it its particular colour. This STOP is seldom found to cover the whole range of the keyboard, because its characteristics are much more pleasing in the tenor and treble registers than in the bass. It is also unnecessary for any 'breaking back' in this STOP. Some of the STOPS listed in the above heading 'FLUTES' may be combined to form a CORNET (8. 4. 2⅔. 2. 1⅗). The French term *Cornet décomposé* is used for this combination.

REED CHORUSES have a different function from the basic organ-tone of the DIAPASONS, being used, in the case of the SWELL organ, to bolster the DIAPASONS of the GREAT, and, in the case of the GREAT organ, for powerful climaxes.

Other COMPOUND STOPS are the Sesquialtera 2 RANKS (12. 17) and the Tertian (17. 19). The Acoustic, or Harmonic Bass 32', is an example of the use of combined harmonics forming a resultant tone. Two ranks of pipes may be used (16' and 10⅔') to give the effect of a 32', thus saving space and expense of a full-length 32' rank. However, the result is not as effective as the real thing.

MAKING YOUR FIRST SOUNDS

is probably best that you try out all the STOPS for yourself discovering
he sort of sound they make, if any sound at all in certain cases. If you hold
own Middle C on the GREAT (see diag. below) and pull in and out the
ifferent STOPS of that department, you will find that they have differing
ones and volumes, as well as different pitches. It is important that in the
ase of mechanical DRAWSTOPS you draw the stops fully, trying not to
ause them to bang. Try the same again depressing Middle C of the pedals
o discover which stop or stops are connected to the pedals (see diagram
f PEDALBOARD on p.41).

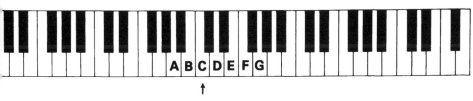

Middle C

Some STOPS do not produce a sound but serve other functions. For
xample 'Swell to Great', 'Positive to Great', 'Great to Pedal', Manual I/II'
re all means of coupling the sounds of the various keyboards and pedals
ogether.

In order to begin, find a fairly soft, yet clear stop on the GREAT which
at 8' pitch (a suitable stop may be the Stopped Diapason 8', Gedact 8'
r the Rohrflute 8', but if your organ has none of these, try to find a soft
quivalent on the GREAT). The combination of STOPS in use at any one time
known as the REGISTRATION.

1 Manual playing *

SOME BASIC EXERCISES

Draw an 8' STOP on the GREAT, clear and precise in sound, but not too loud
(e.g. OPEN DIAPASON). Take care that you approach the keys with a good
hand position in order that each finger is able to play with equal weight.

*Chapters 1 and 2 may be studied simultaneously.

Make a point of playing and releasing the key precisely, without hitting it hard, but playing firmly enough to push the key down fully. When playing, each finger should move up to but not more than 1″, and the movement should be from the knuckle. Make certain not to move the wrist, arm or shoulder at this stage. In the beginning, be sure to keep a steady pulse spending about a second on each crotchet. Your wrist-watch may be useful here in establishing the pulse. Gradually increase the tempo to two crotchets per second. It would be a good idea to count out loud occasionally, to check that you are playing with a constant pulse. Play each hand separately at first, ensuring that the hand is held in the position shown in the photograph above. The exercises below may be played in three different ways using the following touches:

i) **staccato** (literally meaning 'detached', but normally associated with short, crisp notes). Keep the hand fairly still and play the keys with the fingertips, as if stroking the key, drawing the finger slightly towards the body. Make sure your nails are not too long! Listen for what is known as the starting transient of each note, more marked in some organs than others. This is the sound made as the full speech of each pipe develops.

ii) **détaché** (in effect, a less separated form of staccato): almost join the sound of each note to the next, leaving a very small gap between the sounds. It should still be possible to hear the starting transient.

iii) **legato** (smoothly): linking one sound smoothly to the next, but without smudging. The starting transient should not be audible with this touch.

Occasionally vary the REGISTRATION trying out different colours (STOPPED DIAPASON or Gamba, or a STOP on the SWELL).

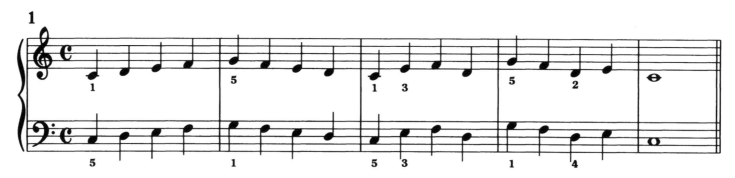

Now transpose this into the following keys: **E** major, **G** major and **B** major, using the same fingering

Now transpose this into the following keys: **D** major, **F** major and **A** major, using the same fingering

Transpose into **D, E, F, G, A** and **B**

Transpose into **Db, Eb, F#, Ab** and **Bb**

CROSSING OVER AND PASSING UNDER

Play with a *legato* touch:

HOLDING NOTES WHILE EXERCISING OTHER FINGERS

Play with a *legato* touch:

Some exercises for strengthening the weaker fingers: play with a *legato* or *detaché* touch

SOME TRILLING EXERCISES

Play with a *legato* touch
right hand:

left hand:

TOUCH, ARTICULATION AND FINGERING IN EARLY MUSIC

Touch

The three contrasting touches described on page 10 are intended to illustrate variety of touch in the broadest terms. They are certainly not the only forms of touch. Indeed, there are infinite gradations which will unfold with experience. How do we determine which touch to play with? Putting to one side the whim of the performer, the answer lies in the period and style of the music concerned. For instance, in the 16th and 17th centuries organists probably played mostly, if not totally, *détaché*, judging from contemporary treatises on keyboard playing. Among these are the writings of the Italian, Girolamo Diruta (1550-1610?) and the Spaniard, Tomás de Sancta Maria (c 1510-70).

Sancta Maria gives a detailed description of the touch he prefers: 'With regard to playing the music with limpidity and distinction of the voices . . . note that for this two things are required. The first and principal is that when one has the fingers strike the keys, the finger that strikes first is always[3] raised [from the key] before the one that immediately follows it strikes – in ascending as [well as] in descending [motion]. And [one] always proceeds in this manner, otherwise one finger will overtake the other. And if one voice overtakes and covers up another, it follows that that which is played [will be] conveyed uncleanly and despicably; and limpidity or distinction of the voices will [thus] not be produced [in the music].'[1]

At the opposite end of the scale we find writings and fingerings from the 19th and 20th centuries by Lemmens, Stainer and Dupré (for example), expressing a preference for *legato* touch.

We know from his biographer Forkel that 'the first thing J. S. Bach (1685-1750) did in his keyboard lessons was to teach his pupils his own kind of touch . . . To this end they had to practise for several months on end nothing but single phrases for all the fingers of both hands, with constant regard for this clear and clean touch.'[2]

There are, however, very few indications in the notation of early music to help us determine which touch to use. Only rarely do we find indications such as slurs and staccato dots, and these sometimes mean different things in early music from Romantic or modern music.[3] The occasional extant slurs and fingerings give us some clues. The Tabulatura Nova of Samuel Scheidt (1624) contains the following examples:

---

[1] *Organ Technique: An Historical Approach,* Sandra Soderlund, Hinshaw Music
[2] *Tercentenary Essays: Bach, Handel, Scarlatti,* Cambridge University Press (article by Mark Lindley, p. 233).
[3] For more details refer to *Keyboard Interpretation,* Howard Ferguson, p.62, Oxford University Press.

Imitatio Violistica

In the first example we may assume that each note was intended to be played for about half its written duration, while the remainder was silent. In the second example we would expect to pair the notes under the slurs together in some form, but it is uncertain as to precisely how *legato* the slurred notes would have been played. Slurs were commonly used by contemporary viol players and sounded 'charming and agreeable' on keyboard instruments.[4] In continuous passage-work the slur indicated the down-bow of a viol player, and would create an accent on the first of each pair.[5]

Here are some rare instances of (*staccato*?) dots above notes in the music of J. S. Bach; the implication being that those notes are to be held for approximately half their usual length.

from Prelude in E♭, BWV 552*

[4] *Bach Interpretation: Articulation Marks in Primary Sources of J. S. Bach*, John Butt, p.53, Cambridge Musical Texts and Monographs.
[5] Ibid. p.91-2.

*BWV = Bach Werke Verzeichnis (Catalogue of Bach's Works) created by Wolfgang Schmieder (1901-73), whose thematic index now provides the standard means of numbering Bach's works.

from Fughetta, 'Allein Gott', BWV 677

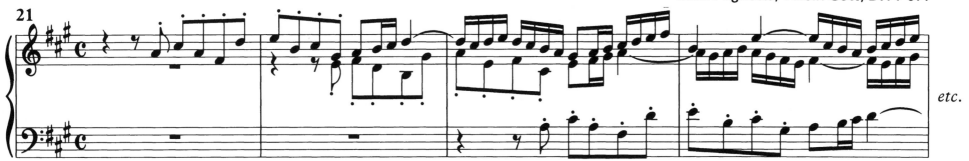

etc.

from Prelude in B minor, BWV 544

etc.

We should, however, generally avoid *staccato* touch when playing contrapuntal music (see **Part-playing** later this Chapter, page 23) because it would be difficult for the listener to follow the direction or line of each part or voice.

Since *legato* touch is more closely associated with Romantic and modern music than with early music, we might, therefore, assume that much early music would have been played with a touch somewhere between *staccato* and *legato*, i.e., with varying degrees of *détaché* touch. Here is what F. W. Marpurg had to say in his *Anleitung zum Klavierspielen*, 1755: 'Opposed to the legato as well as the staccato is the ordinary procedure [touch], in which one releases the finger from the previous key an instant before one plays the following note. This ordinary procedure, since it is always assumed, is never indicated.'[6]

Guillaume-Gabriel Nivers said, in his *Livre d'orgue* (Organ Book) of 1665: 'An important ornament and a sign of good breeding in your performance is a distinct demarcation of all the notes and a subtle slurring of some. This is learned best from singing. To play the notes in a distinct and marked fashion, lift your fingers quickly but not too high. That is, for example, in playing a run of consecutive notes, lift each note promptly as you play the following one, for if you do not lift one until after the next is played, you confuse rather than distinguish the notes. To connect the notes, it is still necessary to distinguish them, but the notes are not released so promptly. This manner is between confusion and distinction and partakes a little of each. It is generally practised with the *ports de voix* [see Chapter 4, page 156] and in certain [other] passages . . . For all these matters consult the method of singing, for the organ should imitate the voice in such things.'[7]

The *cantabile* style of playing features more and more in the late Baroque, with writers about performance encouraging the keyboard musician to think in terms of the human voice. J. S. Bach states on the title page of his Inventions and Sinfonias (2 and 3-part inventions) 'An honest guide . . . to acquire a *cantabile* style of playing'. He also writes *cantabile* at the opening of the Chorale Prelude 'Allein Gott' from the *18 Chorales*. Joachim Quantz, in his *Essay* of 1752, says 'Every instrumentalist ought to try to perform the *Cantabile* as a good singer performs it; and a good singer on his side ought to seek to acquire the fire of good instrumentalists with regard to liveliness, so far as the voice is capable

of it.'[8] It should never be overlooked, however, that in the art of singing, words play their part in articulating and expressing the musical line.

A final word about touch from J. S. Bach's son, C. P. E. Bach, from his *Essay* of 1753[10]; he writes wisely: 'There are many who play stickily, as if they had glue between their fingers. Their touch is lethargic; they hold notes for too long. Others, in an attempt to remedy this, play too short, as if the keys were red-hot. Both are wrong; midway between these extremes is best. Here again I speak in general since every kind of touch is good when used at the proper time.'

Articulation
This is one of the most difficult topics to write about! So much in musical performance depends on an acutely developed ear for detail, as well as an ability to project the music as a whole. Detailed work has to be done in preparation for a performance of even a simple piece of music, but this detail must not become over-apparent to the listener. The art of articulation should be so subtle that the listener is hardly aware of it. Indeed, it should be a secret between the player and the keys. Remember though that 'most problems with articulation . . . remain to be solved without assistance either direct or indirect from the notation' (Diego Otiz, 1553)[11]; that is to say that details of articulation are seldom found in the notation of early music.

Now to try to explain what it is! For an example, let us turn to the flute or recorder. Imagine how dull these instruments would sound without any tonguing or places for taking breaths! All the notes would run into one another without the charm and subtlety of a well-practised tongue-technique or good breath control. The tongue is used to give a slight edge and distinctness to certain notes, and furthermore, it is possible to interpret phrases of music, giving more emphasis and expression through

[6] *J. S. Bach's Keyboard Technique: An Historical Introduction*, Quentin Faulkner, p.39, Concordia.
[7] Soderlund, p.104
[8] *The Interpretation of Early Music*, Robert Donington, p.478, Faber & Faber.
[9] Butt, pp.11-15
[10] *Essay on the True Art of Playing Keyboard Instruments*, C. P. E. Bach (trans. W. J. Mitchell), Schirmer.
[11] Donington, p.477.

articulation to particular notes where required, within the context of the music. Another parallel may be drawn with the bowing of a stringed instrument. A violinist learns to play with a carefully practised bowing technique in order to convey the essence of the music at its best. A fine musical performance often looks easy, but is generally the result of much detailed practice with bowing and fingering.

With the organ, there is no subtlety of breath control required, nor do we play with a bow! The art of achieving niceties of expression therefore is by other means. The fingers are in charge of the 'tonguing' or 'bowing'. Distinctness and subtlety of emphasis and expression are at the organist's fingertips and toes. Above all, the ear must determine the extent of the articulating, and good taste is the overriding governor of such detail. With care and a lot of patience an ordinary row of notes may be transformed into an interesting and compelling line of expressive sounds, mainly achieved by carefully detaching particular notes according to their musical importance, and the effect implied by the composer.

Engramelle, writing in his *Tonotechnie* in Paris, 1775, says: 'All notes in performance . . . have a certain proportion of sound and a certain proportion of silence which together make up the total value of the note. These silences at the end of each note determine its articulation.'[12] These are known as *silences d'articulation*. Engramelle's book concerns the art of pinning cylinders in mechanical musical instruments, and therefore contains valuable historical detail on matters of performance practice.

Fingering
Touch, articulation and fingering (and footing) are inter-related. It helps to gain an understanding of the fingerings and finger-groupings to which composers were accustomed. It will be noticed during the course of this tutor how in Baroque repertoire it is possible to find a relation between the use of strong fingers (especially the middle) and the notes which fall on the important beats, or have an important place in the musical phrase.

In scalic passages fingerings varied considerably. Here is what Johann Mattheson says in his *Kleine general-bass-schule* from 1735: 'One places the middle finger [3] of the left hand upon C, and gently depresses it; then following it, the index finger [2] upon D, as soon as the former has been

released; the thumb upon the E, after the index finger has been released, and thus continues to exchange the index finger and thumb until C has been reached . . .'[13]

Try playing this and some other fingered examples:[14]

from A. Scarlatti:

from Couperin:

[12] Ibid. p.479
[13] Faulkner, p.39
[14] The more common scalic fingerings, generally taught to pianists, may be found in *Play the Organ, A Beginners Tutor.*

from Saint-Lambert:

from Sancta Maria: from Bull:

It will be observed how differently each scale feels, and how easy it would be to play scalic passages clumsily. Remember though that keyboard musicians of the period would have practised these fingering patterns from the very beginning of their study, and they would have felt completely natural to them.

It is well-known that J. S. Bach developed a fingering system making more use of the thumb than before. The system of paired fingerings in scales (e.g., r.h. 2.3.2.3.2.3. and l.h. 2.1.2.1.2.1. – all examples ascending) was gradually supplanted by one involving more passing of the thumb under the fingers, or fingers over the thumb (e.g., r.h. 1.2.3.4.1.2.3.4. and l.h. 5.4.3.2.1.3.2.1.). This gradual shift was due to changing styles of composition in which more extreme keys were used. This inevitably involved more black notes, for which paired fingerings were less comfortable, or even impossible. (The Well-tempered Clavier – The 48 Preludes & Fugues – of J. S. Bach offered the opportunity to play in all keys).

The nature and content of the music, coupled with what we know about playing techniques used by composers themselves, give us strong clues as to how their music was intended to be performed. The following is a short piece called *Applicatio* by J. S. Bach (1685-1750) [15] from the *Clavierbüchlein* (Little Keyboard Book) which he wrote for the education of his eldest son, Wilhelm Friedemann Bach (it should be stressed that this was intended as a simple exercise in the training of a 9-year-old boy!). This contains the only fingering which can be accredited to J. S. Bach. His table of ornaments appears in Chapter 4, page 137-8.

When you first try this piece the result may seem rather clumsy and bumpy, a far cry from the subtle tonguing of a recorder player or the carefully timed bowing of a violinist. The arts of articulating and fingering are acquired gradually over a period of years. Don't expect them to come all at once!

[15] The fingering has been checked at source by Peter le Huray, who believed it to be completely accurate, with the possible exception of bar 2, r.h. top G, where '5' is unclear.

Applicatio in C

A finely balanced and adjusted mechanical/tracker key action is ideal for studying nuances of touch. Such an action, if available to the student for regular practice, will draw him closer to the music and its subtleties, and enable greater finger and foot control. A good teacher will help you to achieve the most from your touch as you progress. Keep in mind that articulations should be sensitive, expressive and subtle and not forced upon the music in a mechanical way, and that fingerings should be tailor-made to suit the natural accentuation of the music.

The following is a short post-Baroque-style piece by Joseph Haydn (1732-1809) in which subtlety of touch is just as vital. It was originally written in 1772 for a musical clock, and should be played on a 4′ FLUTE stop alone. Probably only the slurred pairs of notes were intended to be *legato*. Dwell a little on the 1st beat of each bar, in order to portray the minuet-like character of the piece.

Minuet no.17 from the *Clock Pieces*

[registration: Flute 4′]

J. Haydn (1732-1809)

[♩ = 125]

*The brackets ⌐ and ⌙ indicate that the left hand helps out, and that the part is taken back by the right hand again.

OW TO PRACTISE EFFECTIVELY

he old saying *don't run before you can walk* has to be borne in mind with rgan-playing. If you find yourself playing through the exercises and equently breaking down or faltering, you're playing too fast! Try setting tempo which is very much slower than you have ever imagined possible nd concentrate fully on each note you play. Check that the fingering is dhered to and that your pulse is slow and even. Your aim should be omplete accuracy. Once this is achieved try increasing the tempo radually, ensuring that you do not allow mistakes to creep in. If you find ou are still making mistakes, play at a still slower tempo. You will make ore progress this way than if you were to rush the exercises at this stage.

In the early stages, practising little and often is the most productive. you practise for too long your powers of concentration may decline. you practise only once a week you may find you are spending most of ur time trying to remember what you learnt last week! The most dvantageous method is to practise every day or nearly every day, and ven if you can only manage 30 minutes, you will find that you will quickly ck up from where you left off the previous day. You are then able to hear ur own progress.

Assuming you are able to practise for 40 minutes each day, here is a uggested schedule for the beginner:

    10 minutes: r.h. exercise(s) to be itemized by your teacher
    10 minutes: l.h. exercise(s)
    10 minutes: both hands together, exercise(s)
    10 minutes: pedal exercises

fter a time it should be possible to adjust to an hour each day, as follows:

    5 minutes: r.h. exercise(s)
    5 minutes: l.h. exercise(s)
    20 minutes: both hands together, exercise(s) and pieces
    20 minutes: pedal exercises
    20 minutes: both hands and feet together

ry to plan your practice-time carefully. Do not overdo any one type of xercise. Keep it all progressing gradually, and don't be impatient!

If you still find that you are unable to play accurately at a faster tempo, try picking out short passages which are causing problems and practise them in greater detail. It can help to isolate the offending bars, and to play them through fluently in small groups of notes from the first important note (i.e. on a strong beat) to the first of the next group.

PART-PLAYING

The art of part-playing is one of the most important skills in organ-playing. What is part-playing? It is giving equal emphasis to each voice or part so that it sounds its own musical line (assuming there are two or more voices sounding together) ensuring that each line receives due attention to details of note-value, articulation, phrasing and other nuances.

The number of parts can vary from two (as seen in the following piece) to as many as the fingers and feet can manage, the usual maximum adopted by the Baroque composers being six. Three examples of six-part writing are *Modus ludendi* by Scheidt, the chorale prelude *Aus tiefer Not* by J. S. Bach (BWV 686), and the *Plein jeu* by Michel Corrette (see Chapter 4, page 160) in which the manuals play four-part counterpoint while the pedals play two parts, one for each foot.

During the Baroque era, there is ample evidence of 2-part (Bicinium) being used as teaching material, and the remaining repertoire in this Chapter progresses from 2-part to 4-part compositions.

Try to master the following chorale prelude by Bach at a slow tempo before increasing to the suggested metronome marking. Learn each hand separately at first, and when you feel confident, play with both hands together slowly. The large leaps of the quavers in the l.h. part imply a *détaché* touch, while the r.h. plays *cantabile* (see the definition of *cantabile* earlier in this Chapter, page 18).

Allein Gott in der Höh sei Ehr

[The customary Baroque registration for 'running' basses included the Fagot 16', but care should be exercised with manual 16' REED STOPS on the British organ – they are usually too heavy in sound. There are many alternative REGISTRATIONS for Bicinia. Each hand could be on a different manual, with totally contrasting colours to suit the nature of each part.]

J. S. Bach, BWV 711

The trill may be interpreted in this way:

Befiehl du deine Wege (Commit thy ways to Jesus)

Marpurg is best remembered for his theoretical writings. In this piece of 3-part writing, he cleverly treats the melody canonically, with both upper voices being in a different key. Reference to his views on touch may be found earlier in this Chapter, p.18.
[registration suggestion: Open Diapason 8']

F. W. Marpurg (1718-95)

*In the Preface to his 1968 edition of this piece, Walter Emery suggests that this ornament is unclear and could be intended as a slide:

*probably intended to be played:

In the following chorale prelude by J. S. Bach, known as one of the 'lesser Kyrie Preludes', we meet 4-part counterpoint. In order to maintain the flow of parts, it is often necessary for one hand to help the other, especially where large stretches are involved (e.g. bars 9 and 22).

Kyrie, Gott Vater in Ewigkeit

J. S. Bach, BWV 672

[registration suggestion: Stopped Diapason 8']

Some works have a variable number of parts [voices] during their course. The Prelude from *Prelude and Fughetta in C* (BWV 870a) is an example of this, and is included here as a further example of Bachian fingering (even though it appears in a copy of the piece in the hand of one of Bach's students, J. C. Vogler, and may not be fingered by Bach at all).[16] It is interesting to note the complete lack of finger substitution (i.e. exchanging fingers on a held note, a technique used often in Romantic and modern music, enabling a *legato* move to the next note – see Chapter 5, page 173). Great care should be exercised in playing each line of counterpoint accurately, ensuring that long notes are held at such places as bars 3 and 4.

Prelude, from Prelude and Fughetta in C

J. S. Bach, BWV 870a

[16] It is printed here by kind permission of the estate of Peter le Huray. See also his *Authenticity in Performance*, Cambridge University Press.

* probably 4th finger intended, not 2nd
** the *e′* to be played by the r.h.

Two of Pachelbel's 94 Magnificat versets follow (usually known as 'Fugues on the Magnificat'), also in 4 parts. They were probably intended for use as organ versets at Vespers, alternating with sung chant.[17] The subjects of the Fugues (the subject being the theme on which each Fugue is founded – in these cases the first two bars) do not appear to bear any direct relation to the Magnificat plainchant, but during the course of each Fugue resemblances to the plainsong can be detected here and there.

Mag-ni - fi-cat a - ni-ma me-a Do-mi-num. Et_ ex-ul-ta-vit spi-ri-tus me-us   in_ Deo sa-lu-ta-ri me - o.

Tone I, Fugue no.11

Johann Pachelbel (1653-1706)

[registration suggestion: *Gt.* Flutes 8' and 4', 15th]

[17] *The Organ Music of J. S. Bach (III: A Background)*, p.28, Peter Williams, Cambridge University Press

Tone I, Fugue no.14
[registration suggestion: Gt. to Mixture]

Johann Pachelbel

2 Playing with the feet — pedalling

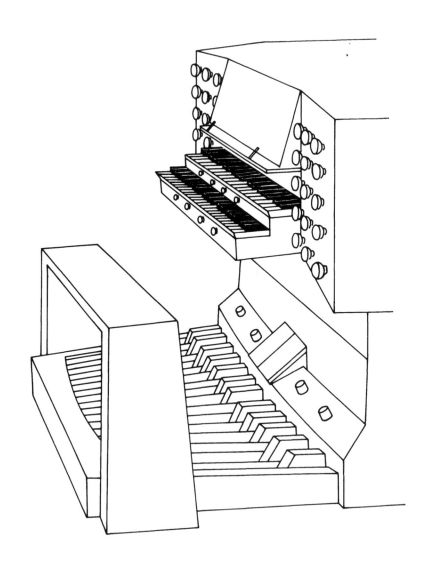

FOOTWEAR

Try to find a pair of shoes which you can set aside solely for organ-playing — it is inadvisable to use the same shoes that you wear for walking in the street. Your playing shoes should be comfortable, as narrow as your foot will allow, and preferably with a slightly worn leather sole. It is possible to use composition soles, but the important thing is that your foot is able to slide fairly easily down the length of the key, while retaining an element of grip when required. A slightly deeper heel than usual can make for more comfortable pedal-playing.

TOES AND HEELS

Two techniques should be mastered: one using the toes only, and the other making use of heels too.[1] There were several treatises on organ-playing from the late 18th and early 19th centuries which advocated learning more than one pedal technique. The constant use of toes and heels, arguably a relatively recent technique, undoubtedly suits Romantic and modern music in which a *legato* line is required much of the time. The toes-only technique is coming back into vogue because it is a vital aspect in striving for authenticity in early music performance. It is believed that Bach, his precursors and his contemporaries played most of the time with toes alone.

The dimensions of their CONSOLES were rather different from those of our time, and it is important to note in broad terms how they varied from present-day CONSOLES. The depth of their pedal keys from the organ bench was greater, and the pedal keyboard was set further under the bench. We can learn from this that they must have played with more pointed toes than is generally suitable for our CONSOLES. We should also note that people were shorter!

[1] For a full discussion on early pedal technique see Williams pp.241-251.

compared with one from the Bach era

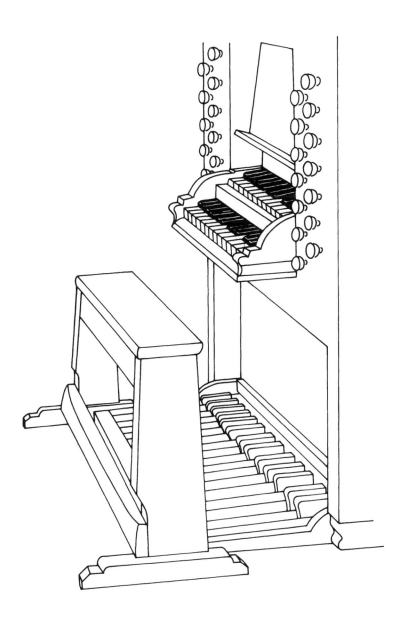

Nowadays, there are basically two kinds of PEDALBOARD, known as 'straight' and 'radiating'; both are sometimes slightly concave, that is, they rise gradually towards each end. Here are two diagrams showing a straight PEDALBOARD and a radiating one.

"Middle **C**" of the pedalboard

This **C** couples up to Middle **C** of the manuals if "Gt. to Ped." coupler is used

Straight Pedalboard

Radiating Pedalboard

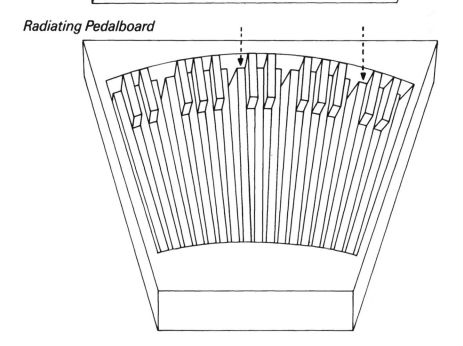

i) Playing with toes only

Here are some general tips:

In the beginning, it is probably a good thing to look down occasionally at the pedals to check what you are doing. However, the ultimate aim is to play the pedals without looking at all, and the earlier you are able to do this the better!

In the exercises that follow, only minimal weight of the leg should be used for pressing down the key. Try to use the ankle joint only.

Shuffling along the seat to reach the extremities should be avoided. Keeping the knees together, swivel slightly from your centre point on the bench to reach these notes.

When playing with the feet alone the hands should grasp the bench firmly.

Try not to cause too much ACTION noise. As with the MANUALS, play the pedal keys firmly enough for precision, but not so firmly that they clatter.

Care should be taken to see that the correct part of the foot is used. Play with the big toe!

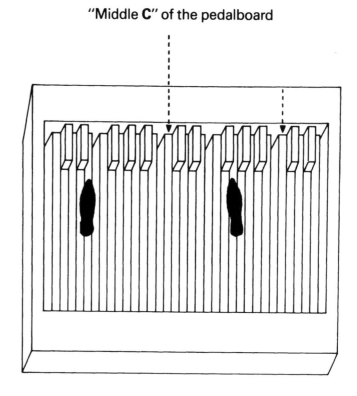

"Middle **C**" of the pedalboard

Right foot playing **G** with the big toe

Left foot playing **E** with the big toe

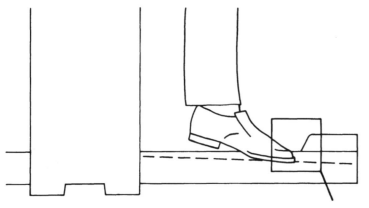

Play within this area

Note the following signs and adhere to them strictly:

V =   to be played by the right toe

Λ =   to be played by the left toe

Play with a *legato* touch:

[registration suggestions (1) Bourdon 16', Principal 8' (2) Bourdon 16', Bass Flute 8', Fifteenth 4' (3) Bourdon 16', Bass Flute 8', Flute 4', (4) Ped. 16' coupled to a combination of stops on the Great.]

this exercise could continue up to top E♭

*J.S. = John Stainer; D.S. = the author; W.G.A. = W.G. Alcock; J.C.H.R. = J.C.H. Rinck

36

this exercise could continue up to top **E**

37

this exercise could continue up to top **F**

This exercise may be transposed into many different keys:

38

39

D.S.

40

W.G.A.

41

Try the following with both *legato* and *staccato* touches:

With a *détaché* touch:

legato:

Play *détaché,* slightly lengthening the right-foot melody notes:

Tallis' Canon, adapted

51

Play the following two exercises from Hamilton's Catechism (1850) with a *détaché* touch, spending slightly longer on the most important beats in each bar:

52

53

6

54

D.S.

...he following three exercises on a 4' STOP. If there is not one available in the pedal department on your practice organ, draw a 4 ...use the Great to Pedal COUPLER. Play with a *legato* touch:

✹   Pass left foot over right   *   Pass left foot behind right

✠   Pass right foot over left

In scalic passages for alternate toes, make sure the toes are well-pointed, and when ascending, pass the left toe over the right, and when descending pass the right toe over the left:

except where accidentals occur:

at ⊘ pass right foot behind left

Pedalling for scales in all keys using toes and heels may be found on pages 51-2.

i) *Playing with heels and toes*

◯ above the pedal stave is to be played by the right heel

◯ below the pedal stave is to be played by the left heel

Play with a *legato* touch:

50

In the following two exercises, play with a *legato* touch under the slurs, and lift the foot off the key when each slur ends:

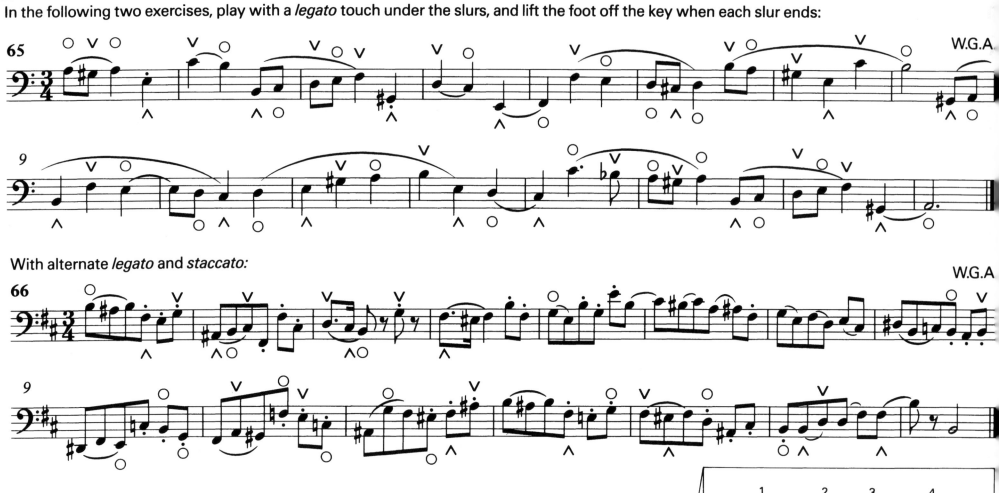

With alternate *legato* and *staccato*:

If difficulty is experienced in finding the starting notes in the exercises without looking at the pedals, study this diagram to see how feeling between the groups of 'black' keys (equivalent to the black keys of the manuals) can help. Gently tap the side of the 'black' keys in the spaces marked 1 to 4, to get your bearings.

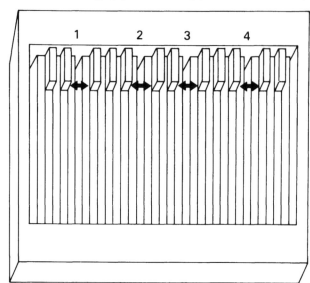

The 12 Major Scales

With pedalling to suit a *legato* touch:

52

The 12 Melodic Minor Scales

With pedalling to suit a *legato* touch:

To end this Chapter, the Pedal-Exercitium, thought to be by J. S. Bach, BWV 598*

registration suggestion: ORGANO PLENO]

*see *The Organ Music of J. S. Bach,* Vol.I, p.319, Peter Williams, Cambridge University Press.

It seems the composer left this unfinished. The small notes and the pedalling have been added by the author.

3 Co-ordination

As a step towards trio-playing and music requiring both hands and feet together, it is necessary to gain independence between the left hand and pedals. If this important study is omitted, there will be great difficulty for the left hand in keeping to its own part. The tendency is for the left hand to move in the same direction as the pedals, instead of playing its own part. Therefore, ensure that sufficient time is spent on these exercises, and that they are practised thoroughly on the lines previously set out, before proceeding to **Simple trio-playing.**

Here is a recommended practice-routine for all exercises and pieces in this chapter. Try to master i and ii before going on to iii, and iii and iv before going on to v:

i   manuals alone
ii   pedals alone
iii l.h. and pedals
iv   r.h. and pedals (where applicable)
v   l.h., r.h. and pedals (where applicable)

Begin very slowly indeed, and do not increase the tempo until complete accuracy and confidence are achieved.

LEFT HAND AND PEDALS

[registration suggestion: *Ped.* Bourdon 16′, Principal 8′; *Gt.* Stopped Diapason 8′, Principal 4′]
legato:

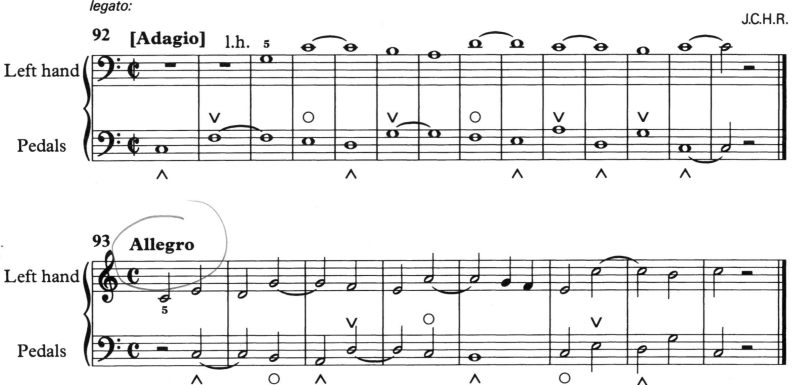

. nand *legato* and the pedals *détaché:*

94 Allegro moderato

Exercises 95 and 96 each have three sections, **a, b** and **c.** In the first, the pedal is identical in all three sections, and in the second, the left hand is identical Vary the REGISTRATION according to the mood of each section, keeping the pedal REGISTRATION independent from that of the left hand, but ensuring good balance between the parts.

Play *legato* under the phrase-marks, and 'take a breath' before the start of each new phrase.

W.G.A.

SIMPLE TRIO-PLAYING

Here we reach the ultimate in independence, with the right hand, left hand and feet each playing a line of music. It will help to think in terms of each line being played by a different instrument. Each part or voice needs to be learned thoroughly before combining it with another. Do not attempt to play all three parts together until all combinations of two parts have been mastered: i.e., left hand and right hand together; right hand and pedals; left hand and pedals, this latter being the most difficult combination for the beginner. Play *legato* under the phrase marks, and 'take a breath' before the start of each new phrase.

[registration suggestion: r.h.: *Sw.* Oboe 8'; l.h.: *Ch.* Flutes 8' and 4' or *Gt.* Flute 8'; *Ped:* soft 16' and 8']

Chorale varied, from Hamilton's Catechism (third edition, 1850).

[registration suggestion: Manuals I and II 8′ and 4′, contrasting stops, but balancing. Pedal at 16′ and 8′, allowing the Chorale to stand out a little]

Try playing the pedals *legato* and the manuals *détaché*:

Variation 2 from Variations on *Liebster Jesu, wir sind hier.*
Rinck was a pupil of Kittel (Bach's last pupil) and Forkel (Bach's biographer) and was renowned for his 'Practical Organ School', opus 55, which comprised
6 volumes. Play with *legato* touch, but ensure that the repeated notes are repeated clearly.
[registration suggestion: Man. I and II Flute 8' (balancing); Ped. Soft 16' and 8']

J. C. H. Rinck (1770-1846)

The trills could be executed as follows:

Nun ruhen alle Wälder, based on a melody by Heinrich Isaak, 1475

[registration suggestion: r.h. *Sw.* Oboe (box closed); l.h. *Ch.* Clarinet (box closed); *Ped.* very soft 8′]

Armin Knab (1881-1951)

Ruhig (*calmly*) [♩ = 40]

Man. I

101

4-PART INCLUDING PEDALS

The hands play on the same manual in this section.

Study no.1 from *12 Studies*

Adolf Hesse was probably a pupil of Rinck and Forkel. From 1831 till his death he was organist at Breslau, and in 1844 he opened the new organ at Saint-Eustache, Paris, astonishing the Parisians by his pedal-playing. His *Practical Organist* contained 29 pieces. Among his pupils was the influential Belgian organist and teacher Nicolas Jacques Lemmens (1823-81).

[registration suggestion: *Gt.* Diapasons 8′, 4′; *Ped.* 16′, 8′ to balance]

Adolf Hesse (1809-63)

Prelude no.1 in C from *Thirty Preludes in all the major and minor keys*
[registration suggestion: *Gt.* 8′ 8′ 4′ 2′ *Ped.* 16′ 8′ 8′ 4′ to balance]

J. C. H. Rinck (1770-1846)

Andante, opus 15, no.9

Gustav Merkel studied in Dresden and became organist at two churches there before becoming Court Organist in 1864. He wrote works mainly for the organ and piano, including an *Organ School.*

[registration suggestion: *Sw.* 8′ 8′ 8′ 4′ *Gt.* 8′ 8′ *Ped.* soft 16′ 8′, Sw. to Gt., Sw. to Ped.]

Gustav Merkel (1827-85)

t may be preferred not to use the Swell pedal until Chapter 7 has been studied.

**This sign (⌐⌐) means play alternate toe and heel with the same foot.

Andante, no.1 from *Nine Short Pieces*
[registration suggestion: *Sw.* 8′ 8′ *Gt.* 8′ and 4′ (Flutes); *Ped.* 16′ 8′, Sw. to Ped., Sw. to Gt.]

Gustav Merkel

*Again, it might be preferable to study Chapter 7 before using the Swell pedal.

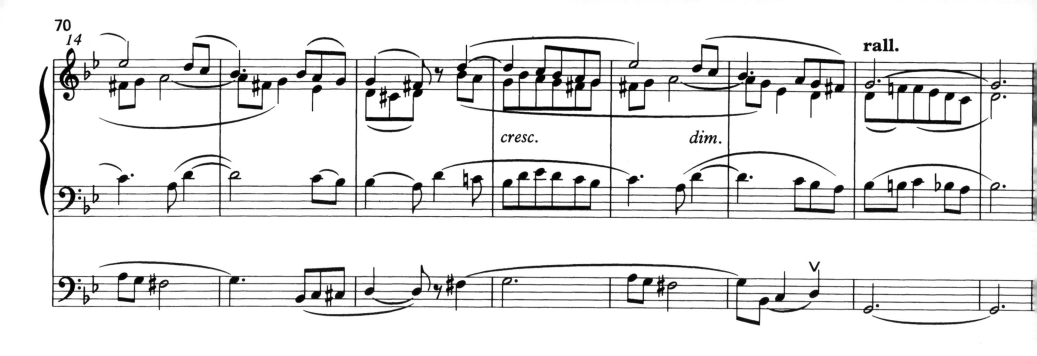

Prelude no.2 in A minor from *Thirty Preludes in all the major and minor keys*
[registration suggestion: *Gt.* 16′ 8′ 8′ 4′ *Sw.* 8′ 4′ and Oboe box ½ open. *Ped.* 16′ 16′ 8′, Sw. to Gt., Sw. to Ped., Gt. to Ped]

J. C. H. Rinck

*probably intended to be played thus:

Prelude no.8 in F sharp minor from *Thirty Preludes in all the major and minor keys*

[Try working out a registration scheme yourself, satisfying the dynamic markings.]

J. C. H. Rinck

*Here is the first point in this Tutor in which alternate sides of the same toe are used. Try to achieve a good *legato*.

It may also be treated as an exercise:

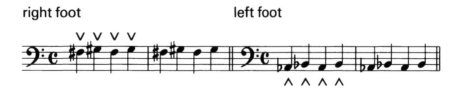

Registering trios

There are several Trio REGISTRATIONS in G. F. Kauffmann's *Harmonische Seelenlust*, published in Leipzig between 1733 and 1736 and undoubtedly known to J. S. Bach[1]. According to Kauffmann very little UPPERWORK (i.e. high-pitched STOPS) was in vogue in Trio REGISTRATIONS around that time. Here are two examples:

1. r.h. Prinzipal 8′
   l.h.   Principal 4′ (played an octave lower)
   ped. Subbass 16′, Oktavbass 8′

2. r.h. HM (i.e. Hauptmanual) Prinzipal 8′
   l.h.   OW (i.e. Oberwerk) Clarin 4′ and Spillpfeife 4′ (or Prinzipal 4′) – played an octave lower
   ped. Subbass 16′, Oktavbass 8′

The use of the Prinzipals in trios is interesting, especially considering that the 'werk prinzip' style of organ-building (see Chapter 4, p.118) prevalent in the Baroque dictated similar dimensions and scaling for those stops. They were often almost identical in tone and volume, though independent from each other by their differing location within the instrument. An interesting point is that when the left hand plays one octave lower than printed, the position at the console is more comfortable than otherwise.

Much care is needed when registering trios on the British organ. It is often impossible to achieve an ideal balance between the parts. Try at first with 8′ stops in the manuals (not necessarily with similar tone colours) and add 4′ stops if necessary. In the pedals try to find a supportive bass for the manual combination, preferably at 16′ and 8′ pitches. It may be necessary to couple the pedals to one of the manuals, preferably a manual independent of those being used by the hands.

Part of *Jesu, meine Freude*
[registration suggestion: see above]

---

[1] *J. S. Bach as Organist*, p.210 ed. Stauffer and May, Batsford   *A possible interpretation of the trill:

Second movement from Concerto per la Chiesa by G. P. Telemann (1681-1767), arranged for the organ by J. G. Walther (1684-1748).
Telemann, Bach and Walther were all colleagues, the latter two being cousins. It was common practice for composers to copy or rearrange another's works. After all, it was a means of learning the art of composition. The following movement is from Walther's arrangement for the organ of Telemann's Concerto, probably written, in this instance, for no other reason than to make an ensemble work available to solo organists, a valuable work he did with many Italian string concertos. It is not strictly a trio in the sense of three single voices; it is more an ensemble trio-sonata texture, in which more than three voices appear occasionally.
[registration suggestion: see p.74]

Possible interpretation of the trills and mordent:

Schmücke dich, O liebe Seele*

[registration suggestion: see p.74]

F. W. Marpurg

*There is no tempo indication given by the composer. As this piece is being used as a learning exercise, it would be sensible to begin at a slow tempo and gradually increase to ♪ = 100 if possible, or even ♪ = 120, but it is difficult at this latter tempo.

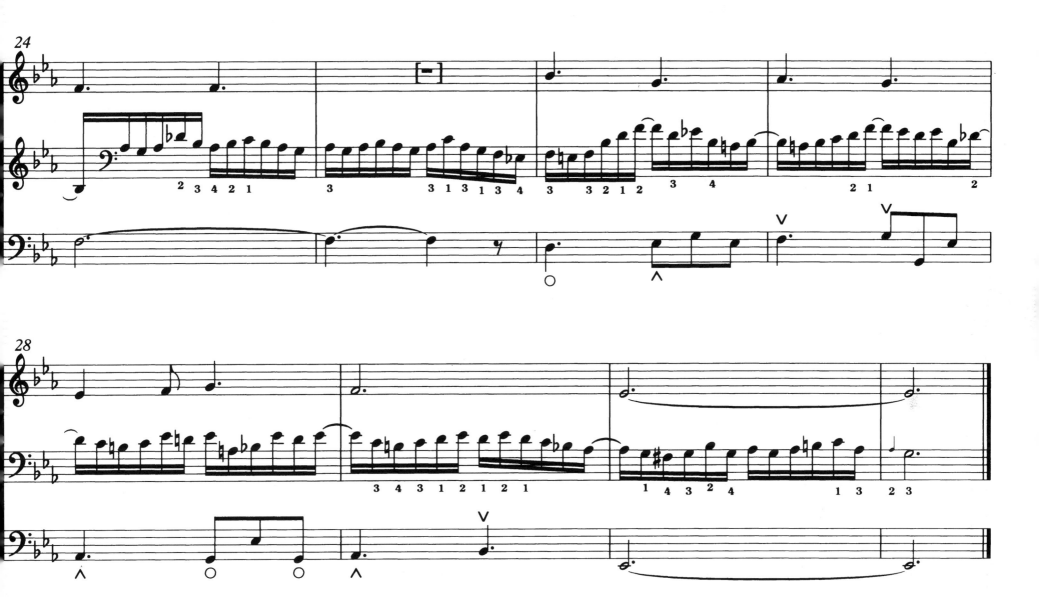

Inventio in C a 2 Clav. and Pedal

Gerber was a pupil of J. S. Bach in Leipzig from 1725-27. In 1731 he became court organist in Sonderhausen and while he was there he composed
Six Inventions for the organ (1737). He was also a skilful instrument maker and invented some unusual ones.

[registration suggestion: see p.74]

111 [Moderato] [♩ = 76]

H. N. Gerber (1702-75

*No pedalling is inserted here, because the author feels that the all-toes technique and a *détaché* touch is the most appropriate. The student should aim at alternate toes wherever comfortable.

**In the Preface to her edition of 1973, Susi Jeans states: According to the practice of the time, slurs were usually written only in the first few bars; it was left to the performer to apply them in corresponding passages. Trills were often treated in the same way. In the source it is often impossible to say whether the slurs

are placed thus: 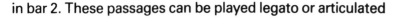 or or

Bar 1 lh. MS has only the slurs; the dots are printed by analogy with the first half of bar 38 — which incidentally shows that *in this theme* the slurs cover two notes, not three. The quavers should be played *détaché*.

Bar 4 rh. Here, as at bars 7, 30, and 34, the MS slurring is reproduced as literally as possible. The unusual slurring is probably a cancellation sign for the articulation

in bar 2. These passages can be played legato or articulated

Bar 9 rh. In the MS, the fifth note is e², with no accidental. See bars 6, 22, and 29. Either bar 9 must have d² (not e²), or it must have ♭e² — in which case bars 6, 22, and 29 are all wrong.

Inventio in A minor a 2 Clav. and Pedal

H. N. Gerber

*The author prefers a *détaché* touch in the pedals, but feels there is no good reason to avoid the occasional heel in this piece. He has therefore only marked those places where a heel could be appropriate.

Possible interpretation of the cadential trills:

Trio in F, opus 49, no.10

[registration suggestion: Man. I and II, balancing 8' and 4', Ped. 16' 8']

Josef Rheinberger (1839-1901)

Andante molto [♩ = 65]

113

Man. I

Man. II *espress.*

Trio in D flat, opus 49, no.4 (for one or two manuals)
[registration suggestion: Man(s) 8′ and 8′, Ped. 16′ and 8′]

Josef Rheinberger

114 **Allegretto quasi Andantino** [♩ = 63]

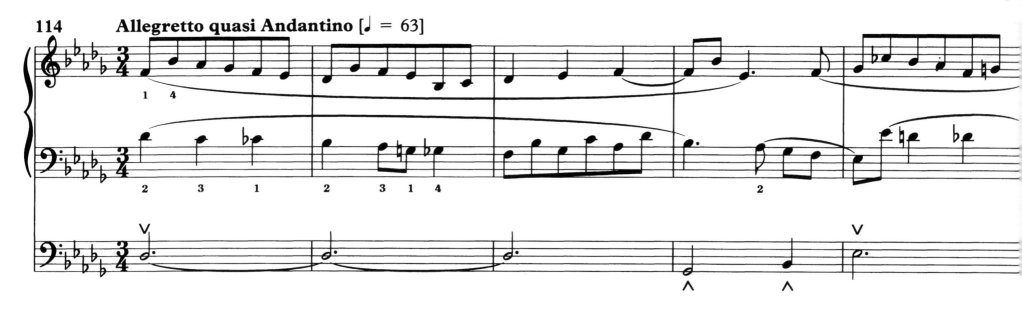

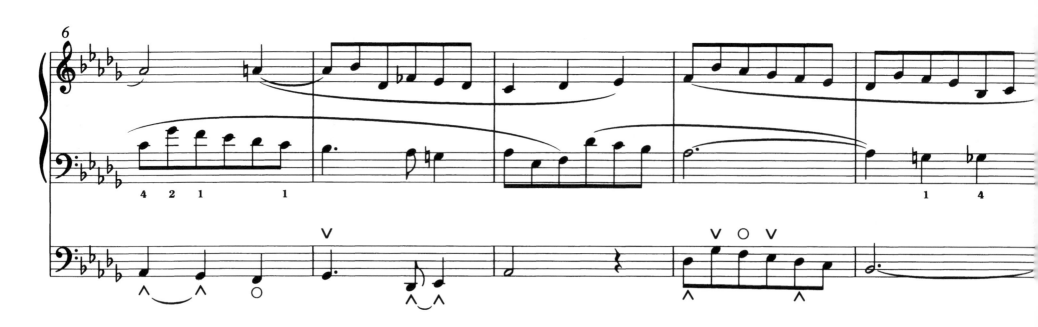

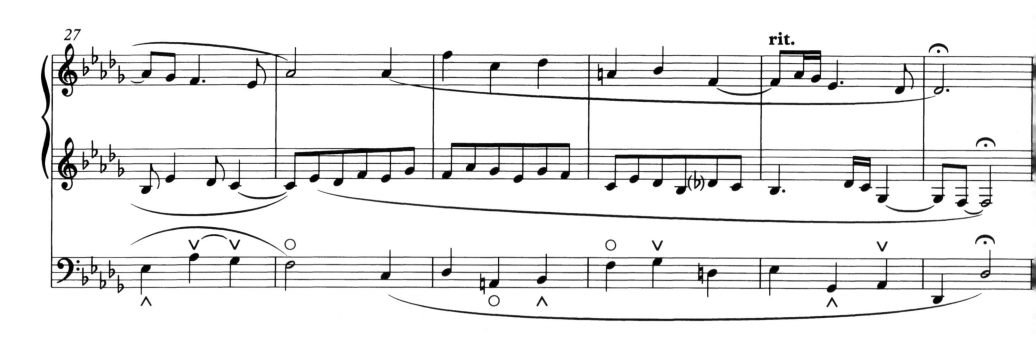

rtödt uns durch dein' Güte ('Mortify us by Thy goodness')

[registration suggestion: r.h. 8′ 4′; l.h. 16′ 8′; ped. 4′ (reed?)]

J. S. Bach arr. C. H. Trevor

[Andante con moto] [♩ = c.60]

(l.h. *détaché*)

*It is suggested that this piece be regarded by the student as a self-fingering and footing exercise, guided by the teacher. The first few are given for guidance.

4 A study of three different organ-playing traditions

It will become apparent to the serious student that the organ and its repertoire evolved in different ways in different countries, depending on the requirements of the liturgy and the inventiveness of organ-builders. This chapter looks at three traditions which, up to a point, grew independently of each other, and between which there was surprisingly little interaction. Other traditions may be studied elsewhere.[1]

BRITAIN: FROM THE 16th CENTURY TILL THE 19th CENTURY

The organ of the 1500s and its music

During the course of the 16th century, German organs were gradually developing and adding different departments (werks), including pedal organs. There are examples of organs from the 16th century and before still playing today, even if in somewhat altered forms. In Britain there is evidence that there had been organs for several centuries before the 1500s, but the form they took is a matter for some conjecture as the few surviving details are confusing. What is clear is that the organ was in decline as an instrument during the 1500s, largely due to the Dissolution of the Monasteries (1536), together with Puritan pressure to stem the use of the organ in church services.

It is likely that the average instrument consisted of one manual with a DIAPASON CHORUS, the equivalent of our present-day STOPS at 8', 4', 2⅔', and 2' pitches, sounding a major 3rd lower than our organs today. Most RANKS were probably duplicated (i.e. two pipes to each note) for greater power.

In the first six decades of the century organ music was chiefly *chant* based, serving to alternate with vocal performances of the same chant. From the beginnings of the Reformation (1559) the organ ceased to have a strictly liturgical function and freer forms of writing began to evolve. However, composers still chose to write for the instrument on chant-based themes, even if they were not acceptable for liturgical use. Gradually the organ began to become associated with the Psalms, to interlude between the verses and perhaps occasionally to accompany them.

The most important composers of organ music from the Renaissance were John Ambrose (fl. 1520-45), John Redford (d. 1547), Richard Allwood (fl. 1550-75), William Blitheman (c. 1525-91), Thomas Preston (d. 1559), Thomas Tallis (1505-85), William Byrd (1543-1623), John Bull (1563-1628), Thomas Tomkins (1572-1656) and Thomas Weelkes (c. 1575-1623). Some of the different forms of organ composition from the 16th century are: organ settings of the Mass, In Nomine, Felix Namque, Gloria Tibi Trinitas, Voluntary (the first examples date from about 1550), Verse and Fantasia (Fancy).

Keyboard music covered a wide variety of instruments: the spinet, virginals, harpsichord or organ, and it is frequently left to the organist to decide which works sound most appropriate on his instrument. A clue can be found in the nature of the part-writing. The Fitzwilliam Virginal Book contains a remarkable collection of keyboard works from the Elizabethan era. A passage such as:

[1] *The Faber Series of Early Organ Music* offers a wide range of repertoire. See Chapter 10 for details.
[2] Stephen Bicknell, 'The organ in Britain before 1600 – some observations', *British Institute of Organ Studies Journal*, 5

from a Praeludium by John Bull suits the virginals more than the organ, whereas the Fantasia of Byrd, in the same collection, is infinitely more suited to the organ, an instrument able to sustain its more vocally characterized lines.

The following piece was probably composed by Benjamin Cosyn (1572-1652) in view of the fact that the initials B.C. appear at the end of the manuscript. This manuscript is in the hand of William Ellis, organist of Eton College from about 1620, and of St. John's College Oxford until the Commonwealth. Not much is known about Cosyn except that he was organist at Dulwich College from 1622-24, and at the Charterhouse from 1626 till the Commonwealth. He is chiefly remembered for his Virginal Book which is one of the principal sources of English keyboard music from the Golden Age.

Cosyn himself is known to have added ornaments in his own works and in others' to the point of proliferation. The performer is therefore at liberty to add ornaments in the following, and should refer to **Ornamentation** later in this Chapter on page 117 for guidance.

Verse

[registration suggestions: *Gt.* Diapasons at 8′ and 4′, or 8′ 4′ 2′, or 8′ 4′ 2⅔′ and 2′]

Benjamin Cosyn, (1572-1652)

The development of the second manual

The second manual began to develop around 1600, together with repertoire suited to two keyboards known as Double Voluntaries. These contained solo lines usually in the bass and often ornate in character, accompanied by the softer second manual. In many pieces from the period one finds markings for *Soft organ* and *Loud organ*, or *Single* and *Double*, meaning *Chaire* and *Great*.

From the following list of composers of Double Voluntaries it can be seen that it was a popular form of composition for a long time: John Lugge (1580-c. 1647), Orlando Gibbons (1583-1625), Richard Portman (d.c. 1655), Christopher Gibbons (1615-76), Matthew Locke (c. 1622-77), John Blow (1649-1708), Henry Purcell (1659-95) and William Croft (1678-1727). An example of a Double Voluntary by Blow appears on page 107.

Thomas Dallam built an organ for Worcester Cathedral (1613-14) with the following specification[3]:

GREAT ORGAN		Probable pitch
Two open diapasons	(metal)	8'
Two principals	(metal)	4'
One recorder	(metal, stopped pipes)	8'
One twelfth	(metal)	$2\frac{2}{3}$'
Two small principals or fifteenths	(metal)	2'
CHAIR ORGAN		
One principal	(metal)	4'
One stopped diapason	(wood)	8'
One flute 'unison to the principal'	(wood)	4'
One small principal or fifteenth	(metal)	2'
One two-and-twentieth, or 'squealers'	(metal?)	1'

1612/13 saw the first attempt at printing music from engraved copper plates. *Parthenia,* as it was called, contained 8 pieces by Byrd, 7 by Bull and 6 by Gibbons. It remained the only volume of printed music for solo keyboard for the following 50 years.

The destruction of organs

Civil War broke out in 1642 and one year later the Westminster Assembly overthrew the Elizabethan Church Settlement. 1644 saw the Lords and Commons ordinance 'for the speedy demolishing of all organs . . . in all Cathedralls, and Collegiate or Parish Churches and Chapels'. The wave of Puritanism under Oliver Cromwell's Protectorate swept through the country almost completely destroying the organs.

[3] from *The Complete Keyboard Works of John Lugge* – Novello

The Restoration of the monarchy

Charles II came to the throne in 1660 and great efforts were made to restore the cathedral services as soon as possible. From that time, organs were rebuilt or newly built in places of worship and we begin to find influence from the continent in their specifications. The Dallam family, who had fled to Brittany by November 1642, returned home to work, and the German Bernard Schmidt, later known as Father Smith, came to work in Britain after ten years working as an organ-builder in Holland. Hence we find for the first time in England specifications containing MIXTURES, REED STOPS and CORNETS.

Here is a typical 2-manual Restoration scheme built by Smith for Durham Cathedral in 1685[4]:

GREAT ORGAN

		Probable pitch	
Open diapason	(metal)	8′	54 pipes
Open diapason	(metal)	8′	54 pipes
Stop diapason	(wood)	8′	54 pipes
Principall	(metal)	4′	54 pipes
Holfluit	(wood)	4′	54 pipes
Quinta	(metal)	2⅔′	54 pipes
Super octave	(metal)	2′	54 pipes
Block flute	(metal)	2′	54 pipes
Small quint	(metal)	1⅓′	54 pipes
Mixture	(metal)	3 ranks	162 pipes
Cornet	(metal)	4 ranks	96 pipes
Trumpett	(metal)	8′	54 pipes

CHAIRE ORGAN

Stop diapason	(wood)	8′	54 pipes
Principal (in front)	(metal)	4′	54 pipes
Holfluit	(wood)	4′	54 pipes
Super octave	(metal)	2′	54 pipes
Voice humana	(metal)	8′	54 pipes

(this latter stop being a reed stop, often spelt *Vox humana*)

[4] from *Father Smith*, Andrew Freeman and John Rowntree, Positif Press.

Here is an impression of its casework:

Durham Cathedral (East Front before 1847)

The Restoration voluntary

The earliest voluntaries to be published were by Matthew Locke in his *Melothesia* (1673). The Double Voluntary was beginning to expand to include solos for the right hand as well as the left. Also the form comprising a slow, chordal introduction to a fugal allegro became popular, and remained so for a century and a half. The important composers from the Restoration were Christopher Gibbons (1615-76), Matthew Locke (c. 1622-77), John Blow (1649-1708), Henry Purcell (1659-95) and William Croft (1678-1727).

The following piece is an example of a Double Voluntary from the Restoration, by John Blow. He was organist at Westminster Abbey from 1668 until 1680, when he stepped down from that position in favour of his pupil, Henry Purcell. The ornamentation appropriate to the Restoration should be carefully studied – see under **Ornamentation** later this Chapter (p.117)

A Double Voluntary

[registration suggestion: *Ch.** Stopped Diapason 8′, Principal 4′, Super Octave 2′; *Gt.* Open and Stopped Diapasons 8′, Principal 4′, Twelfth 2⅔′, Fifteenth 2′ (+ Mixture, and/or Trumpet 8′, if not too strong for the accompaniment)]

John Blow (1649-1708)

On some modern organs it may be necessary to use the SWELL instead of the CHOIR.

'Full Organ Cho[rus]' should be interpreted in the context of the Restoration organ (see p.110)

Towards the end of this piece there is a proliferation of ornaments and the student attempting this style for the first time may prefer to omit some of them.

The 18th century voluntary

French influence can be traced in the musical products of the Restoration, probably according to the taste of Charles II cultivated during his time at the French Court at Versailles. But Italian influence was to have a profound and lasting effect on English music, especially during the first half of the 18th century. The late Baroque concerto-style was imitated by organist/composers, and the superficiality of the fast movements was not without its critics. In a much less complicated way than French composers, the English began writing voluntaries containing several movements, and often listing specific stop combinations.

The development of the Echo and Swell

It is unknown precisely when the third keyboard first appeared (known as *Echo*), but its presence in England was evidence of another aspect of continental influence following the Restoration. By the 1670s short-compass Echo departments were built (from Middle C upwards). Their pipework was completely enclosed in a box giving a distant sound. But it was not until 1712 that the first 'swelling' device was introduced, somewhat crudely taking the form of a nag's head rope and pulley. This was at St. Magnus the Martyr, London Bridge, and it was built by Jordan and Son.

From that time, very few Echos were built, the preference being for the SWELL, with the opportunity to play more expressively.

Some registrations explained

Many writings are to be found on the subject of REGISTRATION in the 18th century, two of the most important being by John Marsh (1791), *A Complete Treatise on the Organ*, and Jonas Blewitt (1794), *Preface to his Eighteen Voluntaries*. They all seem to agree on certain broad principles. With regard to the marking 'Full organ', the CORNET STOP should not be included, because that is a SOLO STOP, but the term seems to have several different possible meanings, including the implication that one should play on the GREAT organ. Here are the interpretations of 'Full organ' as listed by Marsh and Blewitt[5]:

up to Sesquialtera
up to Furniture
up to Trumpet
up to Furniture and Trumpet
up to Clarion (with Trumpet)
(all presumably 8' 8' 4' 2⅔ 2' as well)
The CORNET should not be used with the Full Organ.

As manual 16' stops were uncommon in 18th century England, it follo that the above combinations would have been based at 8' pitch. Here some other STOP combinations frequently found in 18th century org music, together with some probable explanations:

Diapasons: the GREAT OPEN DIAPASON 8' and Stopped Diapason 8' dra together, a combination commonly used for slow, introduct movements. Occasionally the more specific registration 'Diapason' is n with. This could be an indication of the gradual development of the o DIAPASON in terms of increased volume and support for the chor without the Stopped Diapason being necessary.

Flute: the FLUTE 4' of the CHOIR, generally used as a solo register a probably played at the pitch written (i.e. sounding an octave high together with a suitable accompaniment on the GREAT (e.g. Stopp Diapason 8').

Ecchos: played on the 'Echo' (or SWELL, presumably with the box clos on the corresponding solo combination to that used on the GREAT.

Full Swell: the right hand alone playing on all the stops available (s specification below) but without the SWELL CORNET STOP, while the l hand accompanies on a suitable REGISTRATION on the GREAT or CHOIR.

Trumpet: the Trumpet stop of the GREAT organ would have be accompanied by the left hand on the CHOIR organ, and the *pia* passages would have been for the 'Ecchoes' or SWELL organ. O 1-manual organ there were often half STOPS provided, e.g. Trumpet Tre and Trumpet Bass, in which case a Trumpet Treble solo could accompanied by a bass combination without the Trumpet Bass, and v versa.

5 *Journal of the British Institute of Organ Studies*, Vol.13, p.26

Cornet: a virtuoso solo for the CORNET stop of the GREAT organ (its pipes were usually 'mounted' on a separate windchest above the GREAT organ), with the left hand accompanying on a balancing registration on the CHOIR organ. On a 1-manual organ there were often half stops provided, e.g. CORNET Treble and Sesquialter Bass, in which case a CORNET Treble solo could be accompanied by a bass combination without the Sesquialter, and vice versa without the CORNET.

Notable 18th century composers included Thomas Roseingrave (1688-1766), Maurice Greene (1696-1755), William Boyce (1711-79), John Stanley (1712-86) and George Frederick Handel (1685-1759). Regrettably, Handel wrote very little solo organ music, but his 16 Organ Concertos compensate for that; indeed, he is said to have invented the Organ Concerto.[6] They were intended as interludes between the acts of his oratorios, with Handel himself playing and improvising the solo parts. Typical of the instruments on which he played was the one-manual organ at Covent Garden Theatre, built by Jordan:[7]

Open Diapason 8', Stop Diapason 8', Principal 4', Twelfth 2⅔', Fifteenth 2', Tierce 1⅗', Trumpet 8' (compass G,-d''' 55 notes)

The following piece is a Cornet Voluntary by John Robinson (1682-1762) in which the renowned agility of his fingers might have been displayed, using this colourful solo stop together with its echo counterpart. In 1712, Robinson was the first person to play publicly on an English organ possessing Jordan's 'swelling' device (see before, p.110).[8] He became organist at Westminster Abbey in 1727, a post he held until his death. There is no place where 'swelling' is called for in this piece. The registration would have been along the following lines:

Slow introduction: *Gt.* Open Diapason 8', Stopped Diapason 8'

Andante: r.h. *Gt.* Cornet 5 ranks
l.h. *Ch.* Stopped Diapason 8', Principal 4' (or other balancing combination, taking care not to drown the echo registration)
r.h. *Echo* Stopped Diapason, Principal 4', Cornet III

In the absence of a proper CORNET STOP, another combination may be possible of STOPS comprising those pitches which go to make up the CORNET (i.e. 8', 4' 2⅔', 2' and 1⅗', usually of wide-scaled flute character). Where even these are not available, FLUTES at 8' and 4' pitches together with a Nazard 2⅔' or twelfth 2⅔' (providing it is not too strong) will suffice, with the echo played on the SWELL 8', 4', 2⅔' and/or Oboe with the box (nearly?) closed. On a two-MANUAL organ, the echoes may be played on the same keyboard as the accompaniment.

[6] *English Keyboard Music Before the 19th Century*, p.203, John Caldwell, Blackwell.
[7] from the Preface by Peter Williams to his edition of Handel's Organ Concertos, opus 7, Oxford University Press.
[8] *The Story of the Organ*, p.139, C. F. Abdy Williams, Walter Scott.

[Cornet] Voluntary in A minor

[registration suggestion: see before]

John Robinson (1682-1762)

The ornaments could be interpreted along the following lines:

Both hands were probably intended to be played with some form of *détaché* touch. The author prefers the l.h. part to be considerably more *détaché* than the r.h..

The development of pedals

The earliest sets of pedals merely pulled down the lower keys of the GREAT manual, and rarely had independent pipes. These pedals were known quite simply, as 'pull-downs'.

The organ that Father Smith built for St Paul's Cathedral between 1695 and 1697 is generally recognized as being the first British organ to have had pedals fitted (in 1720?), although there were no independent pedal pipes. The Harris organ built in 1722 for St. Mary Redcliffe, Bristol was probably the second organ to have pedal pull-downs[9]. However, there is new evidence to suggest that the organ of Adlington Hall, Cheshire had pedals as early as 1693[10]. What is abundantly clear is that the pedal department was slow to develop in Britain, and it probably did not become fully established until the Great Exhibition of 1851 which featured organs by British builders demonstrating their latest inventions. It was not until 1880 that standard measurements for PEDALBOARDS were agreed at the Royal College of Organists. These remained standard for nearly a century.

Compass of the keyboards

The Great Exhibition was also responsible for the standardization of the manual compass to the German norm (i.e. from **C**, as found today). The compass prior to that usually extended below **C**, often incorporating a SHORT and sometimes a BROKEN OCTAVE. The Echo, and subsequently the SWELL, was frequently of short compass, the former usually extending down to Middle **C** only, while the SWELL gradually extended downwards over the years.

A 3-MANUAL specification follows of the organ at York Minster after repairs effected in 1803 by Green & Blyth[11]. It was originally built by Robert Dallam in 1634, and was one of the few that escaped destruction during the Civil War:

GREAT ORGAN – GG (no GG #) to e‴

Open diapason (No.1)	8′	57 pipes
Open diapason (No.2)	8′	57 pipes
Open diapason (No.3)	8′	57 pipes
Stopped diapason	8′	57 pipes
Principal	4′	57 pipes
Nason	4′	57 pipes
Twelfth	2⅔′	57 pipes
Fifteenth	2′	57 pipes
Sesquialtera	3 ranks	171 pipes
Mixture	3 ranks	171 pipes
Cornet (from c′)	4 ranks	116 pipes
Trumpet	8′	57 pipes
Clarion	4′	57 pipes

SWELL ORGAN – f to e‴ (i.e. F below middle C to E)

Open diapason	8′	36 pipes
Stopped diapason	8′	36 pipes
Dulciana	8′	36 pipes
Principal	4′	36 pipes
Principal Dulciana	4′	36 pipes
Cornet	3 ranks	108 pipes
Trumpet	8′	36 pipes
Hautboy	8′	36 pipes

CHOIR ORGAN – GG (no GG #) to e‴

Stopped diapason	8′	37 pipes
Dulciana (from Gamut G)	8′	46 pipes
Principal	4′	57 pipes
Flute	4′	57 pipes
Fifteenth	2′	57 pipes
Bassoon	8′	36 pipes

PEDAL
Keys to C [PULL-DOWNS]

[9] *The British Organ* p.82 Clutton and Niland, Batsford
[10] *Journal of the British Institute of Organ Studies*, Vol.10, p.66
[11] from *The Organ*, Vol.V, p.197

Ornamentation

The student will soon become aware that much organ music, especially early music, is quite heavily ornamented or embellished. Far from being a chore, the study of ornamentation, if meticulously practised, can be delightful and rewarding. It should be kept in mind that ornamentation exists to beautify the music, and is a subtle and charming vehicle of expression.

The topic is vital, but complicated, with great tomes written about it![12] There are even different realizations of identical signs according to the country of origin and date of composition. The serious student, sooner or later, will want to delve into the subject in greater detail, and for this purpose tables of ornaments appear during the course of this tutor relevant to the playing traditions discussed.

Most British keyboard compositions prior to the Restoration (1660) have only two signs for ornaments, and they appear almost haphazardly, possibly suggesting that the interpretation of ornaments was left mostly to the taste of the performer. There are very few extant British tables of ornaments. The earliest is attributed to Edward (Elway) Bevan (c.1550-?1637), (British Library, London Add. MS 31403). Here it is as a guide to some of the possible embellishments of the Renaissance:

Writing in 1959, John Steele, who edited some other Voluntaries believed to be by Cosyn, comments along the following lines about pre-Restoration ornamentation: 'leading-notes at cadences were usually ornamented with a trill . . . the Virginalists often wrote these out in full:

On the note D # particularly, an ornament would have been desirable to disguise the 'wolves'[13] caused by mean-tone temperament, the usual contemporary tuning. Other places where ornaments seem necessary are dotted-note figures, e.g.

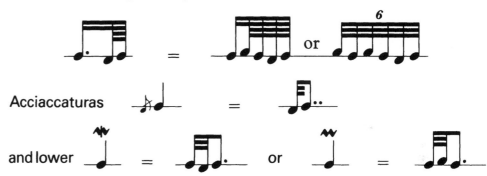

upper mordents may be inserted as the player deems fit.'

The most important Restoration table of ornaments for the keyboard player appears in Purcell's *A Choice Collection of Lessons for the Harpsichord or Spinet* (1696). There is some controversy as to how they should be interpreted! Some writers claim that the table was incorrectly published at the outset. It is published below in its original form, because there is a possibility that it is correct as it stands.

[12] Notably *Ornamentation in Baroque and Post-Baroque Music,* Frederick Neumann, Princeton
[13] Wolves are extremely out-of-tune intervals, which occur in certain unequal temperaments, and which cause a howling effect.

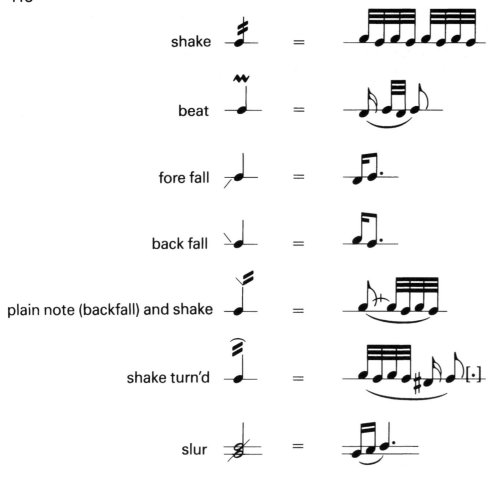

shake

beat

fore fall

back fall

plain note (backfall) and shake

shake turn'd

slur

observe that you always shake from the note above and beat from the note or half note below, according to the key you play in.

Tables of ornaments almost exclusively present trills with equal note values, showing which notes are involved in the trill concerned. But a true and expressive realization will allow an *accelerando* in most cases (see *L'art de toucher le clavecin* (1716) by Couperin) or even a *rallentando* as requested by Frescobaldi at his cadences (preface to his Toccatas, published in Rome, 1614). While following the outline of notes carefully, the student should in the long-term aim at an expressive rendition of ornaments with a freedom which it would not be possible to notate with equal note values. In the beginning, however, a measured approach may be the easiest, while other aspects of technique are being mastered.

NORTHERN AND CENTRAL GERMANY: THE BAROQUE (TILL 1750

Brief historical background

During the 16th century, the continental organ underwent refinement and enlargement, reaching its artistic and musical peak in the High and Late Baroque (1650-1750). French, Italian, Dutch and German organs were quite far apart in sound but not in ideals. They inspired musical master pieces by composers such as deGrigny, Frescobaldi, Sweelinck and above all, J. S. Bach. Indeed, it could be argued that the organ and its music have slowly declined from this era, gradually assuming a more orchestra nature.

The striking difference between the North German Baroque organ and the equivalent British organ is the inclusion of a pedal department, and a complete one at that! There were often as many STOPS in the Pedal as in the Hauptwerk (GREAT) and it was, therefore, quite unnecessary to use pedal couplers to achieve good tonal balance between hands and feet Many organs did not even possess pedal couplers. Therefore, when choosing registration for Baroque works on the British organ, an attempt should be made to achieve an independent, tonally balanced pedal registration, preferably without the use of pedal COUPLERS, or alternatively, the pedals coupled to a different MANUAL from that, or those, being used by the hands.

The most common style of organ-building was known as the 'Werk Prinzip', in which each department (or 'werk') was given its own wooden casework (or 'house') of back, sides and roof. Each 'werk' was based on a Prinzipal RANK (equivalent to the OPEN DIAPASON) of similar pipe-scaling many of whose pipes were used in the facade. Thus, in a 3- or 4-MANUAL and pedal organ, each division would have had Prinzipals at the following pitches:

3-manual		4-manual	
Pedal	16′	Pedal	32′
Hauptwerk	8′	Hauptwerk	16′
Rückpositiv	4′	Rückpositiv	8′
Brustwerk	2′	Oberwerk	4′
		Brustwerk	2′

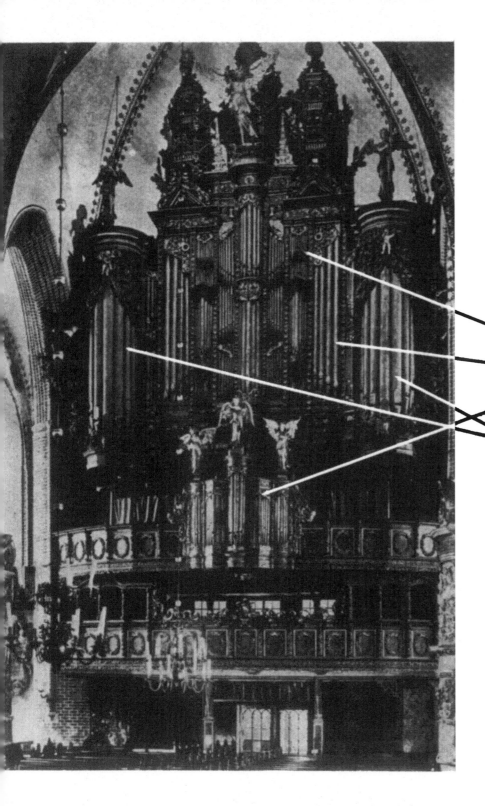

The same concept was also sometimes applied to smaller organs. The effect produced a similar dynamic level and cohesion of tone throughout the organ through the unity of the Prinzipal STOPS. Ideally the organ was placed in the west gallery position, ensuring unhindered egress of tone. The 'geographical' location of each department gave opportunity for contrast and colour, but when coupled they would complement and enrich each other, giving a broad spread of organ tone throughout the church.

It is often possible to trace the history of an old organ from the additions that have been made over the centuries. Here is a photograph of the organ in the Johanniskirche, Lüneburg, built in 1552, showing the Pedal towers which were added 160 years later:

Oberwerk ⎫
Hauptwerk ⎬ from 1551-2 by H. & N. Niehoff
Rückpositiv ⎭

⎰ Pedal towers added
⎱ 1712-14 by Matthias Dropa

Two specifications are reproduced here. The first[1] is that of the large organ as renovated by Johann Friedrich Besser (1670) for St Catharine's church in Hamburg (subsequently destroyed), and known to be an organ admired by J. S. Bach.

[1] from *The Registration of J S Bach's Organ Works,* pp.91 and 346, Thomas Harmon, Uitgeverij Frits Knuf B.V.

WERCK (i.e. HAUPTWERK)

1.	Principal	16'
2.	Quintadena	16'
3.	Bordun	16'
4.	Octava	8'
5.	Spitzflöte	8'
6.	Querflöte	8'
7.	Octava	4'
8.	Octava	2'
9.	Rausch-Pfeiffe	II
10.	Mixtura	X
11.	Trommete	16'

RÜCK-POSITIV

1.	Principal	8'
2.	Gedackt	8'
3.	Quintadena	8'
4.	Octava	4'
5.	Blockflöte	4'
6.	Hohlflöte	4'
7.	Quintflöte (1⅓')	1½'
8.	Sifflet	1'
9.	Sesquialtera	II
10.	Scharff	VIII
11.	Regal	8'
12.	Baarpfeiffe	8'
13.	Schallmey	4'

BRUST

1.	Principal	8'
2.	Octava	4'
3.	Quintadena	4'
4.	Waldpfeiffe	2'
5.	Scharff	VII
6.	Dulcian	16'
7.	Regal	8'

OBER-WERCK

1.	Principal	8'
2.	Hohlflöte	8'
3.	Flöte	4'
4.	Nasat (2⅔')	3'
5.	Gemshorn	2'
6.	Waldflöte	2'
7.	Scharff	VI
8.	Trommete	8'
9.	Zincke	8'
10.	Trommete	4'

PEDAL

1.	Principal	32'
2.	Principal	16'
3.	Sub-Bass	16'
4.	Octava	8'
5.	Gedackt	8'
6.	Octava	4'
7.	Nachthorn	4'
8.	Rauschpfeiffe	II
9.	Mixtura	V
10.	Cimbel	III
11.	Gross-Posaun	32'
12.	Posaune	16'
13.	Dulcian	16'
14.	Trommete	8'
15.	Krumhorn	8'
16.	Schallmey	4'
17.	Cornet-Bass	2'

ACCESSORIES

Tremulants for HW and RP
2 Cymbel Sterne
Tympani
Bird-song
Couplers: HW to Ped.; all manuals to the HW
Ventils for each division

There were many organists connected with Hamburg; among them Heironymus and Jakob Praetorius, Matthias Weckman, Vincent Lübeck Johann Mattheson and Georg Philip Telemann. A movement from Telemann's Concerto per la Chiesa appears in Chapter 3, p.77. At S Catharine's church itself, Heinrich Scheidemann succeeded his father in about 1625, and was in turn succeeded by his pupil Johann Adam Reincken in 1663, who remained until his death in 1722 – 59 years!

The second specification[2] is of a 2-manual organ drawn up by J. S. Bach at the beginning of his last decade. It was built by Trebs in 1742/43 in Bad Berka, near Weimar.

HAUPTWERK		BRUSTWERK (= OBERWERK)		PEDAL	
1. Principal	8'	1. Principal	4'	1. Subbass	16
2. Quintadena	16'	2. Quintadena	8'	2. Principalbass	8
3. Flöte	8'	3. Gedackt	8'	3. Hohlflöte	4
4. Gedackt	8'	4. Nachthorn	4'	4. Posaune	16
5. Gemshorn	8'	5. Quinte	2⅔'	5. Trompete	8
6. Gedackt	4'	6. Oktave	2'	6. Cornet	4
7. Oktave	4'	7. Waldflöte	2'		
8. Quinte	2⅔'	8. Tritonus (= Terz 1⅗)			
9. Nasat	2⅔'	9. Zimbel	3 ranks		
10. Oktave	2'				
11. Sesquialtera	2 ranks				
12. Mixtur	5 ranks	Manual and Pedal			
13. Trompete	8'	couplers			

From about 1700 the Rückpositiv began to fall out of fashion in Centra Germany, but it was still found in Northern Germany and Holland unt well into the 19th century. North and Central German organs of the 18th century tended towards 'the fusion into a continuous ensemble sound which suggests the possibilities of dynamic shadings and graded dynamics. UPPERWORK, especially strong MIXTURES, was replaced by STOP of fundamental pitch, and REED STOPS decreased in number.'[3]

[2] *J. S. Bach as Organist,* p.18, ed. Stauffer and May, Batsford.
[3] *Geschichte des Orgelspiels und der Orgel-komposition,* 3rd ed. Vol.2 pp.969-74, Berlin: Merseburger, 1966.

Some composers and their music

A study of the growth of organ music through the Baroque era cannot fail to reveal that many composers owed their training to Jan Pieterzoon Sweelinck (1562-1621) from the Protestant Netherlands and Girolamo Frescobaldi (1583-1643) from Rome. It was common practice for composers to copy other composers' works, in order to study them, to become more familiar with them, and to have them for their own use. Organ performance and compositional techniques were often handed down from father to son. The following table shows the most important composers for the organ (and one or two others to complete the picture) up to and including J. S. Bach. The French composers listed are those whose works were most likely to have been known to J. S. Bach. The continuous arrows show teacher/pupil links, while the dotted arrows show close colleagues and friends.

Organ music has naturally been very closely linked with the Liturgy, the greater part of earlier music being written for performance at the Mass. This took the form of settings based on a cantus firmus for the purposes of alternating with chanting (alternatum), and Toccatas as preludes during the elevation, or as postludes.

It was for forms devoid of chants that Johann Jacob Froberger (1616-67) became influential, following on from and developing models of his teacher, Frescobaldi. Although writing in some Italianate forms, Sweelinck further influenced the north German tradition by writing many works which were chant or chorale based. Indeed, it is generally accepted that he invented the chorale with variations.

Sweelinck's influence reached many through those who travelled to Amsterdam to study with him; among them Jacob Praetorius (1586-1651), who became organist at the Petrikirche in Hamburg from 1604, Heinrich Scheidemann (1596-1663), who succeeded his father as organist at Katharinen-kirche, Hamburg in about 1625 and Samuel Scheidt (1587-1654), who spent most of life in Halle, becoming organist at the Moritzkirche, and providing future generations with his famed Tabulatura Nova, published in Hamburg in 1624. This was particularly noteworthy for its modernization of musical notation, leaving behind the old German system of tablature (essentially a form of writing music with letters, numbers or other signs, as an alternative to staff notation).

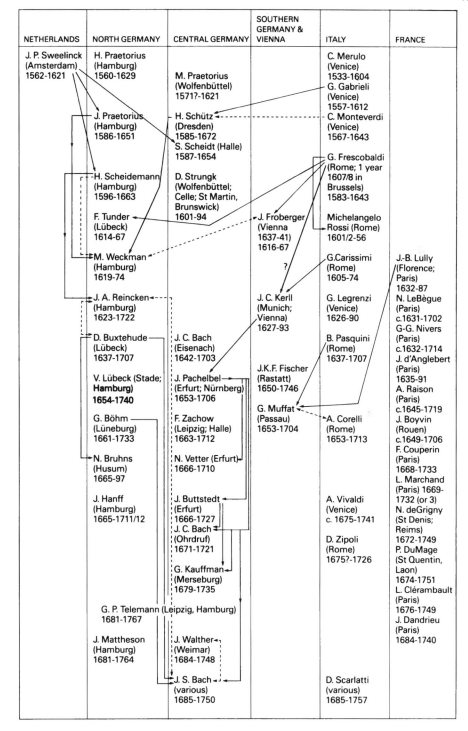

The following piece is part of a non-chorale-based work by Scheidt displaying the Echo style in its most basic form. It is good practice in changing manuals swiftly, without loss of pulse.

Echo Alio Modo

[The registration scheme works best with a 3-manual organ; the l.h. chords on a fairly plain sound (8') and the r.h. alternating between the other keyboards with similar combinations of stops but different dynamic levels (***f/p***). On a 2-manual organ the ***p*** passages have to be played on the same manual as the l.h. accompaniment.

Samuel Scheidt (1587-1654)

Influence from both Italy and the Netherlands reached far beyond those students mentioned earlier (p.121) and various forms can be traced through successive generations of composers to the master of them all, J. S. Bach. The Praeludiums of Scheidemann were often quite short, perhaps reflecting brief preludes or intonations played before and during the Masses. Others were longer, developing different sections, some of a fugal type. Tunder and Weckman followed suit, and Buxtehude was to expand this sectional form, raising it to the same level on which chorale-based works had been held for some time.

Franz Tunder (1614-67), a pupil of Frescobaldi, was organist at the Marienkirche in Lübeck from 1641, and initiated the renowned evening concerts there, known as *Abendmusiken*[4]. These were maintained until 1810. In the following Praeludium in G minor by Tunder some of the Baroque musical figures (*figurae*) are to be found. These were small groups of notes with clearly recognizable contours and rhythmic features. It is common to find one (or more) *figura* featured many times in a single piece. Two in particular will be found here; the *suspirans* (usually but not exclusively associated with 'sighing') and the *corta* or (which some writers suggest was used to denote 'joy'). Many 17th- and early 18th-century theorists left descriptions of the *figurae* which possibly exceeded 150 in number.

[4] see *Dietrich Buxtehude, Organist in Lübeck*, Kerala Snyder, Schirmer Books.

Praeludium

[registration suggestion: Organo pleno (see p.136)]

atthias Weckman (1619-74) was a pupil of Heinrich Schütz (under whom
e sang as a chorister in Dresden) and Jacob Praetorius in Hamburg.
Weckman was appointed organist at the electoral chapel, Dresden in
637, and after other positions he returned there for a time, before taking
o the post of organist at the Jacobikirche in Hamburg, which he held
om 1655 till his death. He had a life-long friend in Froberger, and could
e described as one of the most Italianate German composers of his
neration.

Dietrich Buxtehude (1637-1707) succeeded Tunder at the Marienkirche,
beck in 1668, and to hear and learn from Buxtehude, J. S. Bach travelled
0 miles on foot. The North German Praeludium as exemplified by
uxtehude, was far from standard in form, often containing several
ntrasting movements similar to the form known as the Italian Variation
anzona. The pedals were frequently employed in solo passages, and
citative-like sections had manual flourishes and dramatic harmonies.
epeated-note fugue subjects became a feature of the late 17th century
orth German Praeludium, with well-known examples among the works
Buxtehude, Lübeck, Böhm and Bruhns.

Vincent Lübeck (1654-1740) became organist in Stade, and later at the
kolaikirche in Hamburg (1702). Georg Böhm (1661-1733), held the
sition as organist at Johanniskirche in Lüneburg from 1698 till his death.
e undoubtedly had a hand in J. S. Bach's musical education when Bach
as a pupil at St Michael's school in Lüneburg (1700-c.1703). In 1775,
P. E. Bach wrote to J. S. Bach's biographer, Forkel, that his father 'loved
d studied the works of the Lüneburg organist, Georg Böhm'[5]. A
vourite pupil of Buxtehude from 1681, Nicolaus Bruhns (1665-97),
came renowned for accompanying himself with the organ foot-pedals
ile he played the violin![6] He was organist at Husum from 1689, and
obably many of his compositions are lost.

Ostinato bass forms, the Chaconne (ciacona) and Passacaglia, were
mmon in Italy. German composers, such as J. C. Kerll, Pachelbel and
uxtehude made good use of these . . . not to mention J. S. Bach. Johann
spar Kerll (1627-93) was a pupil of Carissimi in Rome, and possibly
escobaldi too. He held court positions, notably in Munich. He returned
Vienna as organist at St Stephen's Cathedral (1674-7), where Pachelbel
as his assistant, and probably his student. Johann Pachelbel
353-1706) is also noted for his beautiful chaconnes. He was organist

at Erfurt from 1678 and at Sebalduskirche, Nürnberg from 1695. He is
represented in this volume by two Fugues on the Magnificat in Chapter
1, p.35.

By 1750, all the following forms had fully developed among the free
organ works: Praeludiums, Fantasias, Toccatas, Canzonas, Ricercares,
Passacaglias, Chaconnes, (Trio) Sonatas, Preludes and Fugues, and
Fugues alone. Among the chant-based works were Versets and
Variations, while Chorale-based works fell into four groups: Chorale
Fantasias, Chorale Preludes, Chorale Fughettas and Chorale Partitas.

The Chorale Fantasias of Reincken, Tunder, Weckman, Buxtehude and
others were usually of considerable length and often contained sections
with echoes, similar to the earlier echo fantasia form used by Sweelinck
and Scheidt (see earlier this Chapter, p.122). Johann Adam Reincken
(1623-1722), a pupil of Scheidemann, whom he succeeded at
Katharinenkirche Hamburg in 1663 where he remained for 59 years till
his death, was much admired by Bach.

The Chorale Prelude began life as a much shorter piece than the Chorale
Fantasia, probably serving as an introduction to the melody for the
congregation or as an interlude or meditation at an appropriate place in
the service.

In this example by Delphin Strun[g]k (1600/1-94), the complete chorale
melody is used, ornamented only very slightly. He was organist at
Wolfenbüttel, Celle and St. Martin, Brunswick. This latter post he held
for 55 years till his death. He led the field in employing diminution (i.e. small
groups of notes or musical figures taken from the chorale) in
accompaniments. The Chorale melody is more familiar as *Herzlich thut
mich verlangen* (the Passion Chorale), but, according to Mattheson,
twenty four different hymns were sung to this melody.[7]

[5] The New Grove, Macmillan
[6] Ibid
[7] *The Organ Music of J. S. Bach – Vol. III – A Background*, p.284, Peter Williams,
Cambridge University Press

Lass mich dein sein und bleiben

[registration suggestion: r.h. *Gt.* Open Diapason 8′ (No.2); l.h. *Sw.* or *Ch.* – a suitable accompanying stop(s) at 8′ pitch; *Ped.* 16′ and 8′ to balance]

Delphin Strun[g]k (1600/1-1694)

uxtehude and others used more florid figuration, known as coloratura tyle, often illustrating certain colourful words in the text of the chorale vith musical flourishes. This technique became a feature of chorale ettings with frequent decorative passages of great beauty and oignancy.

Other composers of chorale preludes included Johann Nikolaus Hanff 665-1711/12), who was a Thuringian organist with appointments in utin, Riga and Hamburg. Only six Chorale Preludes remain (in the hand f J. G. Walther), with coloratura figures in evidence, and an example may e found on page 140. Among the many taught by Pachelbel are Johann leinrich Buttstedt (1666-1727) who became organist at three different hurches in Erfurt, and Johann Christoph Bach (1671-1721), eldest brother f J. S. Bach. He was organist at Ohrdruf from 1690, and according to . P. E. Bach's obituary notice of his father, he taught J. S. Bach eyboard-playing.

Johann Gottfried Walther (1684-1748), cousin of J. S. Bach and close olleague at Weimar, wrote many Chorale Preludes (see Volume 1). He vas an Erfurter and town organist of Weimar from 1707. A movement y Georg Philip Telemann, as arranged by Walther for the organ, may be ound in Chapter 3, page 77. Georg Friedrich Kauffmann (1679-1735), a upil of Buttstedt, held among other positions the posts of Court organist nd cathedral organist at Merseburg. In 1722 he competed with Bach, nsuccessfully, for the position of Kantor at Thomaskirche in Leipzig. In is *Harmonische Seelenlust* (published between 1733 and 1736) we find robably the largest number of original registrations for chorale settings om the late baroque era. This was the first collection of organ Chorale reludes to appear in print since Scheidt's Tabulatura Nova of 1624.[8]

ohann Sebastian Bach (1685-1750) was also an assiduous writer of horale Preludes, creating monumental collections of them for various ccasions in the church year, and for the musical and religious education f organists. His chorale-based works express the sentiments of their exts in sublime harmony and counterpoint, and with a perfection of form nd compositional technique never reached before or since. The major ollections are:

rgelbüchlein (the Little Organ Book) BWV 599-644
chübler Chorales BWV 645-650

Eighteen Chorales BWV 651-668
Clavierübung part III BWV 669-689, preceded by the Prelude in E flat (BWV 552) and followed by Four Duetti (BWV 802-805) and the Fugue in E flat (BWV 552)
Neumeister Chorales BWV 714, 719, 742, 957, 1090-1120 (only recently discovered)
Kirnberger's Collection BWV 690-713a
Partitas BWV 766-768, 770-771
Canonic Variations BWV 769
plus numerous miscellaneous Chorale Preludes.

The student may find full details of J. S. Bach's life and works elsewhere. Malcolm Boyd's book in the Master Musician Series (published by Dent) is particularly recommended.

Among Bach's pupils were Johann Tobias Krebs (1690-1762) and his son Johann Ludwig Krebs (1713-80), organist at Altenburg Schloss from 1756, Heinrich Nicolaus Gerber (1702-75), court organist at Sondershausen from 1731 (two of his *Inventions* appear in Chapter 3, pages 84-91), Wilhelm Friedemann Bach (1710-84), second child of J. S. Bach, organist at Sophienkirche in Dresden, Liebfrauenkirche in Halle 1746 and Berlin 1774, and Johann Philipp Kirnberger (1721-83). Many of the latter's musical publications were designed to be practical manifestations of his theoretical interests.[9] He regarded Bach as the supreme composer, performer and teacher.

Probably Johann Peter Kellner (1705-72), and Johann Christoph Oley (1738-89) were pupils of Bach. In any case Oley quite likely knew the Bach family because he had a lot of Bach's manuscripts and copies in his possession. He was organist in Aschersleben from 1762 (a work by him appears in Chapter 9 on page 218). One of Bach's last pupils at the Thomaskirche in Leipzig was Johann Christian Kittel (1732-1809) who wrote a 'practical' instruction book for use of the organ in church services (1801-8). He was organist in Erfurt. A Praeludium by Kittel, in which there is evidence of the change in style from the late Baroque to the Rococo of the pre-Classical period, may be found in Chapter 9, page 208.

[8] The New Grove, Macmillan
[9] The New Grove, Macmillan

Some registrations considered

Organo Pleno

Some composers and organ builders left fairly detailed lists of STOPS to be drawn for ORGANO PLENO (Full Organ). This is not the place to list them all,[10] but they all differ slightly, with some general principles emerging. The term means some form of Full Organ. It would most likely have depended on the nature of the music being performed as to precisely which STOPS were drawn, and the individual specification of the organ available. For example, ORGANO PLENO in a small town church would require fewer stops than in the largest cathedrals, in which louder organ tone can be used for longer periods without palling. A minor-key piece of a tragic nature would surely have been less brilliantly registered than a virtuoso major-key piece.

The Plenum of the German Baroque organ was often based on a 16′ Prinzipal on the Hauptwerk, with a full Prinzipal chorus (i.e. 8′, 4′, 2⅔′, 2′ and MIXTURES) above it, sometimes with a similar 8′-based chorus coupled from the Positiv or Oberwerk. The Pedal was often with a strong foundation of Prinzipals (32′) 16′, 8′, 4′ and MIXTURE, together with REEDS at 16′, (8′ and 4′). Many of the late Baroque composers expected great gravity in their registrations, and might well have considered including manual Tierces and Reeds, and possibly fewer MIXTURE stops. About 10 works of J. S. Bach contain some reference to ORGANO PLENO in their titles. There are many other Bach works in which ORGANO PLENO is implied by the very nature of the music.

Among the organ works as a whole, Bach unfortunately left very few other registrations, and two or three of these are mere guidelines. The list is:

Concerto in D minor after Vivaldi (BWV 596) – various directions.
Gottes Sohn ist kommen (BWV 600) – Manual: Prinzipal 8′; Pedal Cantus firmus: Trompete 8′.
Wachet auf! (BWV 645) – Manuals at 8′, pedal at 16′ (probably with 8′ too).
Wo soll ich fliehen hin (BWV 646) – r.h. at 8′; l.h. running bass at 16′; alto Cantus Firmus played by pedals at 4′ pitch.
Ein feste Burg (BWV 720) – Sesquialtera for the coloratura, and Fagotto (probably 16′) for the running bass (a well documented registration from the late Baroque).

Canata 80: *Ein feste Burg* – Pedal Posaune (probably 16′).
Cantata 161: *Komm, du süsse Todesstunde* – Sesquialtera for the Chor Cantus Firmus.

Coloratura registrations

For the decorated Chorale Preludes there were many differ combinations of stops available. Solo combinations in the early Baroc tended more towards sharper combinations, such as Quintadena 8′ Zimbel III ranks, or an 8′ REED together with bright UPPERWORK on Rückpositiv.

Solo REGISTERS common in the late Baroque era are: Hautbois Schalmei 8′, Krummhorn 8′, Chalumeau 8′ (a stop developed by the org builder Gottfried Silbermann), Vox humana 8′ (with Tremulant), 5-RANK CORNET of the Hauptwerk, and the Sesquialtera (2⅔′ and 1³ probably all being used together with a suitable 8′ FLUE STOP (or two). over Germany Tierce combinations were becoming more common the end of the Baroque.

For a discussion on Trio Registrations, see Chapter 3, page 74.[11]

Registering on the British organ

It would be unwise to advise too specifically on the REGISTRATION German Baroque music on the British organ, because not only individual organs differ so much in size, style and specification, but th are frequently poles apart in basic conception. It is best to list some bro guidelines:

1. Listen to any selected REGISTRATION at a distance from the instrum (i.e. with someone else playing), in order to judge matters of balan volume, texture, etc. Judging these matters from the console usu results in undesirable effects.

[10] see *The Registration of Bach's Organ Works* by Thomas Harmon, and ot works.
[11] For a full discussion on registrational practices of the Bach era, see *The Or Music of J.S. Bach, Part III*, pp.154-170, Peter Williams, Cambridge Univer Press.

For ORGANO PLENO, try to select a full, clear chorus, omitting Trombas, and other high pressure REED STOPS such as Tubas, and Ophicleides. Large scale OPEN DIAPASONS are usually ill-advised, owing to their often overpowering qualities. The same applies to Pedal Open Wood stops. MIXTURE STOPS in some Victorian organs were only intended to be used with the REEDS, and do not sound well as the UPPERWORK of the DIAPASON CHORUS (example: BWV 552).

    a. For the Fantasia-type (Stylus Phantasticus[12]) the plenum is probably best in a full, rich combination, including (soft and clear) manual doubles (i.e. 16' stops) and even a pedal 32' FLUE. Normally the British 32' REED is too overpowering for the manual fluework (example: BWV 542).

    b. For the Vivace, contrapuntal-type Prelude (and Fugue) a more selective chorus of brighter UPPERWORK and less heavy foundations would be suitable, together with a pedal REGISTRATION of FLUES and REEDS. The Pedal REEDS are often too heavy for Bach, and the best solution may be to couple the SWELL REED[S] to the pedals (example: BWV 541)

In coloratura Chorale Preludes, the MUTATION STOPS should be carefully selected for appropriate balance, and to see that they blend, especially the solo ventures into the tenor register. An effective solo combination can be Gt. FLUTES 8' and 4' together with the Twelfth 2⅔' (providing the latter is not too strong). Alternatively, a quiet REED STOP will be suitable or just the 8' OPEN DIAPASON alone (example: BWV 731, later this Chapter, page 143).

As a general rule, try not to change registration during the course of a movement, unless there is a complete fermata in all voices. However, there is evidence that North German organists in the 17th century used REGISTRANTS[13]. Changes are justifiable in multi-sectional works, such as the Praeludium and the lengthy Chorale Fantasia.

The use of the SWELL-pedal in German Baroque music would be unidiomatic.

Trio suggestions are discussed in Chapter 3 page 74.

Ornamentation

It is important to understand and to be able to realize the ornaments of the Bach era. For that reason the table of ornaments by J. S. Bach himself is reproduced here. This is not to say that they apply to all composers from the German Baroque (see below). Bach placed this 'Explication' at the beginning of the Clavier-Büchlein (Little Keyboard Book) intended for the education of his eldest son, Wilhelm Friedemann Bach. The student should be aware that Bach himself only intended these realizations as a model, and the number of repercussions and the speed of the ornament, for example, can vary at the will of the performer, within the general shape of the model.

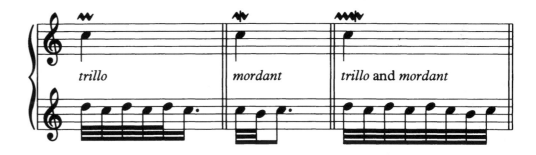

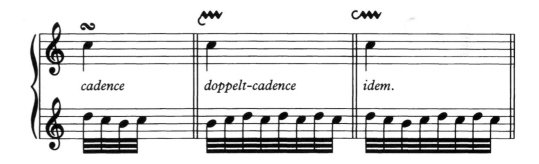

[12] A Baroque term denoting a free style of composition of flamboyant nature. A typical piece in that style contains a chain of contrasting sections, including fugal and cadenza-like passages (see Praeludium by Tunder earlier this Chapter, p.126)

[13] Matthias Weckman. The interpretation of his music, Vol. 1, p.50, Hans Davidsson, Gehrmans Musikförlag; J. S. Bach as Organist, p.36, Stauffer and May (eds.), Batsford

In works of earlier Baroque composers there is often evidence of their customary ornamentation in the music itself. (See, for example Praeludium in G minor by Tunder, earlier this Chapter, page 127, bars 14-16). On other occasions, ornamentation is left to the whim of the performer, especially at cadences. The following variants are possible:

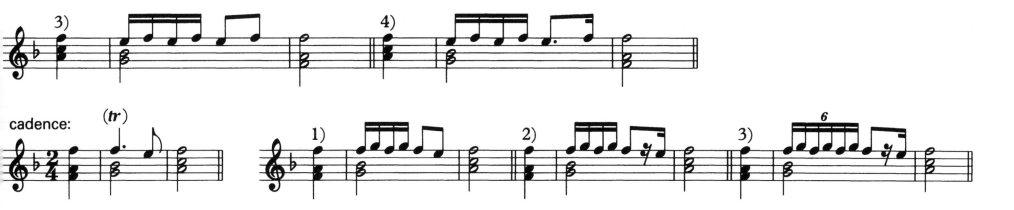

There are many situations in which appropriate ornamentation is implied by the harmony.
For example, at **C** (above) it would be less satisfactory to ornament from the upper auxiliary*, because of the slightly unpleasant accent on the octave Gs on the first beat. It is better to start on the main-note*, as at **C** 1), 2) and 3).

Not recommended:

Worse still, in examples at **C** (above) consecutive octaves are caused when ornamenting from the upper auxiliary*:

It is better to start on the main-note*, as at **C** 1), 2) and 3).

Terminology:

the 'main-note'   the 'upper auxiliary'

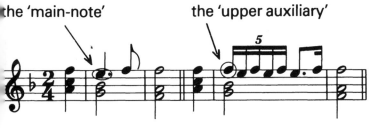

N.B. 'main-note' alternatively known as 'given note' or 'principal note'.

A Chorale Prelude by Johann Nicolaus Hanff (1665-1711/12), fingered and footed in a manner reflecting the fashion at the time, and with som
recommended realizations of the ornaments.

Some ideas about articulation can be gained from a preliminary study of the following extract. Apart from anything else, we need to make the puls
comprehensible to the listener. It would be easy to present the opening as if the first note were placed on the first beat of the bar. Try playing the firs
8 notes attempting to give the idea of the pulse as printed; using the articulations suggested by the thin vertical lines before some notes. Accentuat
the **B** and then the **E**, not by hitting the key harder, because this makes no difference on the organ, but by slightly shortening the length of the note
preceding them. Rests have been inserted at repeated notes, to show how accentuation and clear repetition may be achieved. Please note, thes
are guidelines only.

Now attempt the whole prelude, seeing if you can carry the above suggestions through to the en

Auf Meinen Lieben Gott

[see under **Coloratura registrations** and **Registering on the British organ** on page 136]

Johann Nicolaus Hanff (1665-1711/12)

iebster Jesu, wir sind hier a 2 Clav and Ped.

his Chorale Prelude is typical of the 'coloratura' style, in which the Chorale melody is highly decorated. The r.h. even moves right away from the Chorale t some points.

or registration and ornamentation suggestions see earlier this Chapter, pages 136-7].

J. S. Bach, BWV 731

*probably ♪♪ should be played ♪♪ leaning on the first of the pair.

Prelude and Fugue in E Minor.
This work was probably intended to be played ORGANO PLENO, although the sources do not indicate this. The nature of the writing would seem to suggest the full glory of the Baroque organ, yet in its more doleful sense. See earlier this Chapter, page 136 for a discussion of ORGANO PLENO.

J. S. Bach, BWV 533

FUGUE [♩ = 56]

*At this and similar points the r.h. **B** should be lifted in time for the l.h. to restrike the same note.

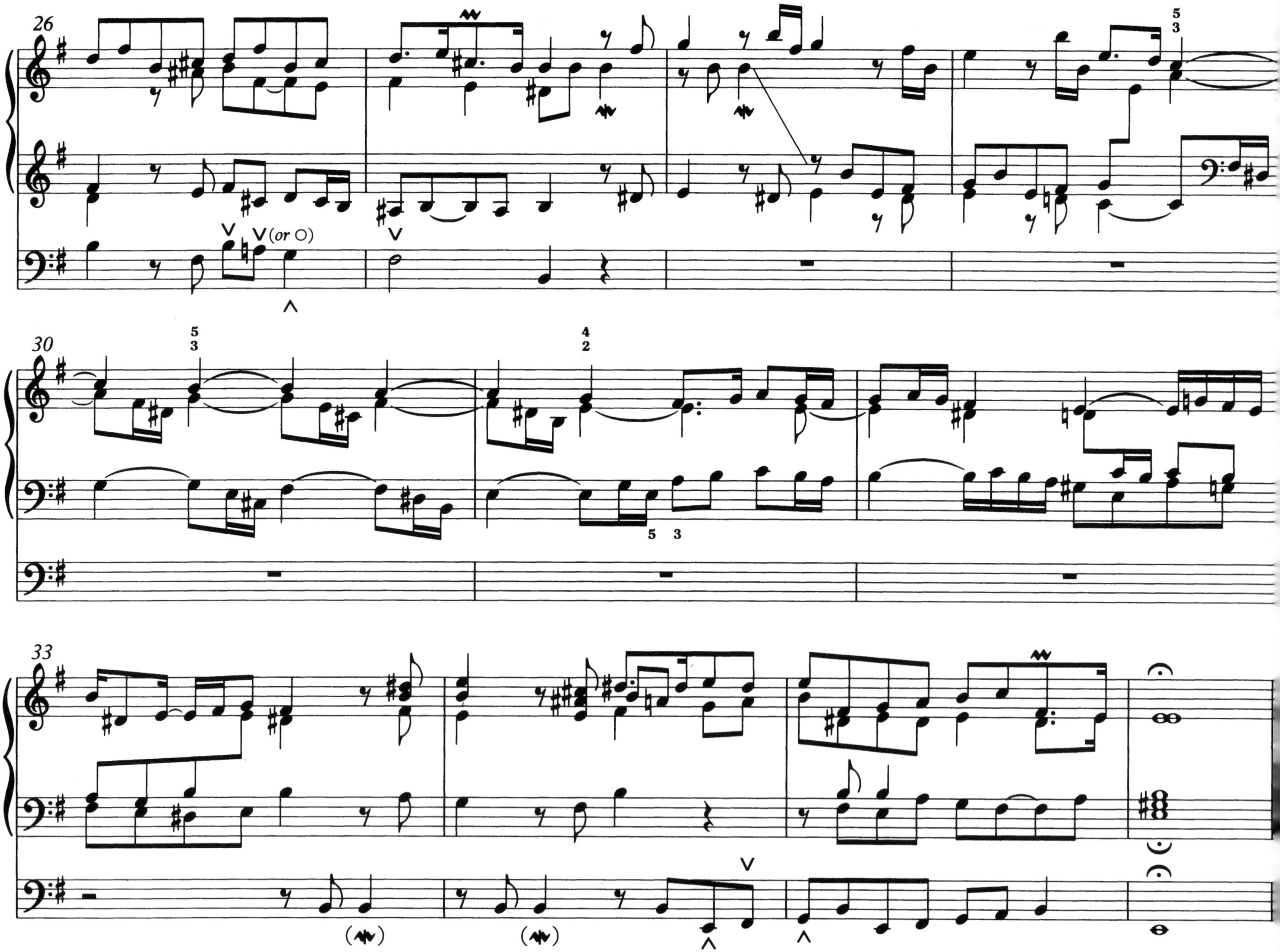
26
(or ○)
30
33

FRANCE: LE GRAND SIÈCLE (c. 1660-1760)

Brief introduction

The French organist/composers of 'Le grand siècle' (i.e. from circa 1660 onwards) were required to play or improvise at certain points in the Mass, alternating with sung chant. Hence there are many settings collated in the Livres d'orgue (Organ Books) which are based on chants used regularly at the Mass. Suites of pieces also emerged with regular patterns of movements and stylized REGISTRATIONS. In addition, ornate and flamboyant settings of Noëls (carols) were popular at Christmas-time in the Parisian churches.

A large French Classical organ could have had a specification along the following lines: [1]

GRAND ORGUE		POSITIF	
Montre	16	Montre	8
Bourdon	16	Bourdon	8
Montre	8	Prestant	4
Bourdon	8	Flûte	4
Gros Nazard	5⅓	Nazard	2⅔
Prestant	4	Doublette	2
Flûte	4	Tierce	1⅗
Grosse Tierce	3⅕	Larigot	1⅓
Nazard	2⅔	Fourniture	III
Doublette	2	Cymbale	III
Quarte de Nazard	2	Cromhorne	8
Tierce	1⅗		
Fourniture	IV	RÉCIT	
Cymbale	III	Cornet	V
Cornet	V	Trompette	8
Trompette	8		
Clairon	4	ECHO	
Voix humaine	8	Cornet	V

Tremblant à vent doux (soft)
Tremblant à vent perdu (strong)

PÉDALE	
Flûte	8
Trompette	8
Clairon	4

Sometimes the Echo had a 'Cornet décomposé' (i.e. you could draw each RANK separately). The term 'Cornet separé' refers to the CORNET whose pipework is placed on a separate chest, i.e. that of the Récit. In the larger organs, the louder stops of the Grand orgue were often to be found on another keyboard, named *Bombarde*.

Some registrations explained

Most composers from this epoch left detailed REGISTRATIONS for their works, and these often differed slightly from one composer to another. However, in broad principle two distinctly different sounds for the full organ developed, known as *Grand jeu* and *Plein jeu*:

GRAND JEU (mostly wide-scaled stops) GRAND ORGUE		PLEIN JEU (mostly narrow-scaled stops)[2] GRAND ORGUE	
(Bourdon	16)	(Montre	16)
(Montre	8)	(Bourdon	16)
Bourdon	8	Montre	8
(Gros Nazard	5⅓)	Bourdon	8
Prestant	4	Prestant	4
(Grosse Tierce	3⅕)	Doublette	2
Nazard	2⅔	Fourniture	IV
Quarte de Nazard	2	Cymbale	III
Tierce	1⅗		
Cornet	V		
Trompette	8		
Clairon	4		

(essentially, these latter three stops form the basis of the *Grand jeu*, together with the Bourdon 8' and Prestant 4')

(continued)

[1] Note that the nearest equivalent French STOP to the German Prinzipal or British OPEN DIAPASON is the Montre, although the German STOPS were usually more forceful, even aggressive, in speech.

[2] The diameter of pipes is referred to as 'scaling'. In general terms the greater the diameter of the pipe the more broad its tone.

POSITIF			POSITIF		
(Montre	8)		(Montre	8)	
Bourdon	8		Bourdon	8	
Prestant	4		Prestant	4	
Nazard	2⅔		Doublette	2	
(Doublette	2)		Fourniture	IV	
Tierce	1³/₅		Cymbale	III	
Cromhorne	8				

PÉDALE			PÉDALE		
Flûte	8		(usually for the Plainchant)		
			Trompette	8	
RÉCIT			(Clairon	4)	

RÉCIT
(short compass – usually from
tenor C)
Cornet   V

ECHO
(short compass – usually from
middle C)
Cornet   V

The *Tremblant fort* (i.e. strong tremulant!) was sometimes used with the *Grand jeu*.

The registers in brackets were those least commonly used in the *Grand* and *Plein jeu*. Probably one of the reasons that two different combinations for full organ developed was because the winding systems did not provide sufficient wind for all the stops together.

The *Tierce en taille* is one of the most beautiful REGISTRATIONS, and inspired some very deeply felt compositions. It literally means 'Tierce in the tenor register', and is always like a recitative in character. Here is the combination as set out in the *Livre d'orgue* of André Raison (1688):

(The following abbreviations are generally used: G.O. = Grand orgue; POS. = Positif; RÉC. = Récit; PÉD. = Pédale)

left hand solo – POS: Montre (i.e. probably implying Prestant 4'), Bourdon 8', Flûte 4', Nazard 2⅔', Doublette 2', Tierce 1³/₅' and Larigot (if there is one).

accompaniment – G.O.: Bourdon 16', Bourdon 8', and 4' (unspecified, but probably Prestant 4') (The Prestant was usually more mildly voiced than the German or English equivalents); PÉD: Flûte 8' (probably with Péd/G.O. coupler).

Many composers left detailed REGISTRATIONS which should be researched by the student and adhered to where the effect is satisfactory. Sadly many printed editions have misleading REGISTRATION directions. In good editions such details are often printed in their Preface. However, on many organs some adjustments are necessary (see below under **Choosing appropriate registrations on the British organ**). Other registrations commonly found in Classical French organ music are:

for the *Fugue:*
G.O. Bourdon 8', Prestant 4', Trompette 8', coupled to POS. Cromhorne 8'

or

G.O. Bourdon 8', Prestant 4', Trompette 8', Clairon 4'

or

POS. Bourdon 8', Prestant 4', Cromhorne 8'

Cromhorne en taille:
accompaniment: G.O. (Bourdon 16'), Bourdon 8', Prestant 4'; PÉD. Flûte 8', (Flûte 4')
left hand solo: POS. Bourdon 8', Prestant 4', Cromhorne 8'. When the G.O. 16' is used in the accompaniment, the Tirasse G.O. (i.e. Gt. to Ped. coupler) should also be drawn.

Basse de Trompette:
accompaniment: POS. Bourdon 8', Prestant 4'
left hand solo: G.O. Bourdon 8', Prestant 4', Trompette 8', Clairon 4'

Récit de Cornet:
right hand solo: G.O. Cornet V
accompaniment: POS. Bourdon 8', Prestant 4'

Duo:
right hand: POS. Bourdon 8', Prestant 4', Nazard 2⅔', (Doublette 2'), Tierce 1³/₅'
left hand: G.O. Bourdon 16', Bourdon 8', Prestant 4', Nazard 2⅔', Quarte de Nazard 2', Tierce 1³/₅'

or

ght hand: RÉC. Cornet V
ft hand: G.O. Bourdon 8', Trompette 8'

io à deux dessus:
ght hand: POS. Bourdon 8', Prestant 4', Cromhorne 8'
ft hand: G.O. Bourdon 16', Bourdon 8', Prestant 4', Nazard 2⅔', Quarte
* Nazard 2', Tierce 1⅗' with Tremblant à vent doux

   or, according to Raison,

ght hand: POS. Bourdon 8', Flûte 4', Nazard 2⅔'
ft hand: G.O. Voix Humaine 8', Bourdon 8', Flûte 4'

eu doux: essentially an accompaniment STOP or combination of STOPS
* suit whichever solo combination is used.

nd d'orgue: G.O. Montre 16', Montre 8', Prestant 4'

oosing appropriate registrations on the British organ

ein jeu
. DIAPASONS 8' to MIXTURES (coupled to Ch. or Pos. to MIXTURE). Take care
t to include the heaviest DIAPASONS or Tierce STOPS. A Double Diapason
' or Bourdon 16' may also be used, where available. REED STOPS at 8' (and
 may be used in the Pedals, if a plainchant bass is in evidence. It may
 necessary to couple REEDS from the SWELL, if the pedal REEDS are too
ong.

and jeu
view of the 'fanfare' nature of this sound it is important to restrict the
GISTRATION to REEDS and wide-scaled FLUES. MIXTURES are not a part of this
GISTRATION! If there is a CORNET STOP, use that (with FLUTES, and especially
e Tierce) together with the most brilliant REEDS (8' and 4'). The PRINCIPAL
is also used in this combination. Tubas and Trombas are usually too
d and dull, and it may be necessary to couple REEDS from the SWELL
tead. At the appearance of a trio section in the movement, composers
ually require one hand to play on the *Cornet separé*, the other on the
sitif *Cromhorne 8'*, while the pedals are on the *Flûte 8'!* In the British
gan the CORNET on a separate CHEST of its own, with its own keyboard,
es not exist. Therefore, the best compromise is often to use the CHOIR
POSITIF cornet décomposé (i.e. FLUTES at 8', 4', 2⅔', 2', 1⅗') as the *Cornet
paré,* while the other hand plays on the Trumpet/Cornopean of the
VELL, with the PRINCIPAL 4'. The French pedal *Flûte 8'* is a wide-scaled

stop of considerable fundamental tone, and frequently the best choice
is the PRINCIPAL 8' (possibly with the Bass Flute 8') for an appropriate
balance, providing the PRINCIPAL is not too loud.

The *Tierce en taille* is problematic, even impossible, if the organ at your
disposal does not have a CHORUS of FLUTES at 8', 4', 2⅔', 2', 1⅗' (and 1⅓').
There is really no alternative other than to select a different combination
altogether or a solo STOP which sounds relatively colourful and
sufficiently doleful. The accompaniment could be on the GREAT (Bourdon
16') STOPPED DIAPASON 8', (and 4' FLUTE) with the Pedal Bass FLUTE 8'
together with another soft 8' if possible, to help give more of the character
of the French *Flûte 8'* stop. When the GREAT 16' is used, the Gt/Ped
coupler should also be drawn.

for the *Fugue:* Gt. STOPPED DIAPASON 8', Principal 4', Trumpet 8'. If this latter
stop is too round or overbearing, try coupling the SWELL Trumpet 8' (and
possibly Clarion 4') instead.

Cromhorne en taille: the closest equivalent solo STOP is probably the
Clarinet 8', although on the British organ this is considerably more
restrained than the French *Cromhorne 8'*. It may therefore be necessary
to pad out the sound with other 8' STOPS, and possibly a 4' FLUTE, too.
Listen carefully to see that they all blend well together. A suitable
balancing accompaniment is required along the lines of the *Tierce en taille*
mentioned above.

Basse de Trompette:
left hand: Gt. STOPPED DIAPASON 8', PRINCIPAL 4', Trumpet 8', (and Clarion 4'),
or if too dull or heavy: Sw. STOPPED DIAPASON 8', PRINCIPAL 4', Trumpet 8', (and
Clarion 4'), plus some other 8' stops to firm it up , if necessary.
accompaniment: FLUTE 8', PRINCIPAL 4'.

Récit de Cornet: This again is difficult to realize, if there is no CORNET STOP
at your disposal. But try the following:
right hand solo: Gt. FLUTES 8' and 4', Twelfth 2⅔' (if this latter is not too
loud)
accompaniment: a combination of 8' and 4' stops on CHOIR or SWELL

Duo: in the event of the organ lacking the equivalent STOPS, to those listed
above on page 152, any balancing combination would be acceptable, and
can often be quite pleasing. Remember to make the organ sound well
in its own right, even if its specification has no Classical French STOPS at
all.

Trio à deux dessus: try the following:
right hand: Gt. FLUTES 8' and 4', Twelfth 2⅔' (if this latter is not too loud)
left hand: Clarinet 8', plus other flues at 8' and 4' pitches.

Jeu doux: essentially an accompaniment stop or combination of STOPS to suit whichever solo combination is used.

Fond d'orgue: Gt. Double Diapason 16' (if too heavy, use the Bourdon 16' instead), OPEN DIAPASON 8', PRINCIPAL 4'.

Some more detailed points about registration

G.O./Péd and Pos/G.O. COUPLERS were sometimes provided, but there is no mention of either COUPLER in the *Livres d'orgue* of Guillaume-Gabriel Nivers (1665), Nicolas LeBègue (1676 and 1678) or Gilles Jullien (1690).

G.O./Péd. and Pos/G.O. COUPLERS are called for by Jacques Boyvin (1689) and André Raison (1688), and Pos/G.O. is called for by Gaspard Corrette (1703) and Michel Corrette (1737).

In the *Grand jeu*, only Nivers and an anonymous author of a manuscript from Tours (c.1710) call for the use of the G.O. 16'.

The 16' Bourdon and/or Montre G.O. accompaniment for the *Tierce en taille* (with implied pedal COUPLER) is called for by LeBègue (1676), André Raison (1688), Lambert Chaumont (1695) and Gaspard Corrette (1703).

However, Jacques Boyvin (1689) calls for the accompaniments to the *Récits* always to be G.O. Bourdon (8') and Prestant (4'), and Michel Corrette (1737) for the accompaniment to the *Tierce en taille* to be on the G.O. Bourdon (8'), Prestant (4') or Montre (8').

Michel Corrette (1737) also calls for the Pedalles de Flûtes (sic.) in which he may be implying the use of Bourdon 16' and Flûte 8' together.

The Anonymous Manuscript from Caen (1746) calls for the Pedal Bourdon 16' and two FLUTES (presumably 8' and 4') in the accompaniments for the *Tierce en taille* (G.O. Bourdon 4', Montre (8')), and for *Les Flûte.* There is also the first mention of a Pedal Bombarde (presumably 16') for the *Grand jeu*, but note how late this work is dated.

The Larigot is used in the *Tierce en taille* combination in all extant instructions except for the Anonymous Manuscript from Caen (1746).

Dom Francois Bedos de Celles claims that he is quoting the most competent and celebrated Parisian organists such as Messiers (sic. Calvière, Fouquet, Couperin, Balbâtre and others in his *L'Art du facteur d'orgues (1766-70)* when he says that the recommended REGISTRATIONS of the older masters have all been improved upon according to the change of taste since their times. We therefore find that many combinations are expanded or exaggerated by Dom Bedos.

The above list is compiled with reference to *The Language of the Classical French Organ* by Fenner Douglass, published by Yale University Press. Further details on aspects of registration may be found in this book.

Inequality (notes inégales)

Inequality is the term applied to the art of interpreting notes which appear with equal value on the printed page with varying degrees of freedom. Although most early western musical traditions incorporated some degree of inequality, the subject was more consistently aired in France than elsewhere, with most composers and theorists leaving instructions for the interpreter. It would be impossible to quote them all here, but some quotations will be used in an attempt to gain a clear picture of how and when *notes inégales* would have been used.

An important statement on the subject from Saint-Lambert: 'The degree of inequality may range from mild and lilting (much like triplet rhythm) on the one hand, to sharp and vigorous (much like dotted notes) on the other hand. It is not the difference of notation, but the musical effect required, which should determine the rhythm in performance. Dotted notes which are under-dotted in performance, and equal notes which are mildly unequalised in performance, sound the same: i.e. lilting. This lilting, triplet-like rhythm is by far the most important and characteristic use of inequality'.[3]

An introduction to the topic can be made by summarizing the broad principles of writers such as Loulié and Saint-Lambert, writing around 1700. This summary should apply to all compositions from *le grand siècle* since it can be confirmed between 1650 and 1800 by some thirty texts.

---

[3] *The Interpretation of Early Music* p.452, Robert Donington, Faber & Faber.

LOURER (the lilting rhythm – giving grace and charm).

when the time signature of a movement is	pairs of notes of the values below generally become *inégales* (long-short)
$\frac{3}{1}$	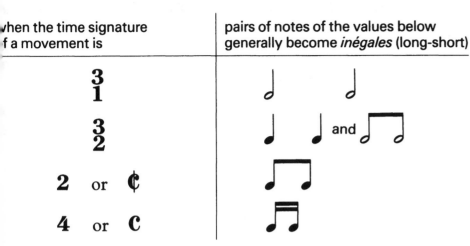
$\frac{3}{2}$	
2 or ¢	
4 or C	

The most usual interpretation is when pairs or lines of conjunct quavers

are played

There are varying degrees of inequality, and if these were to be written in present-day notation, they might look like this

or etc.

The nature of the music should always govern the extent of the inequality, and *le bon goût* (good taste) should be the over-riding arbiter!

There are some exceptions when *notes inégales* should <u>not</u> be used. Here are the most important ones:

i   when a piece has one of the following headings: notes égales, martelées, détachées, mouvement décidé, marqué.

ii   where there is disjunct movement, i.e. a melody with lots of leaps.

iii at syncopated passages, or those with lots of rests.

iv   at repetitions of the same note.

v   where a dot or vertical line is placed above the note:

vi   where a slur covers more than two notes:

vii in fast movements, in which grace and charm would not be in keeping.

2.   COULER (the snapped rhythm) [4]

When indicated by the following signs ♪ or ♪ according to some writers (e.g. Donington)

the rhythm should be altered to ♪. ♪. (short-long)

The term *coulé* is discussed on page 158

[4] The whole question of rhythmic alteration in Baroque music is a very controversial one in some respects; with regard to the *couler* rhythm, it is important to realize the following points:
i   there is only one writer who mentions it as a possible form of alteration (Loulié, 1696)
ii   several writers after him contradict this point.
iii the term *couler* is used by Couperin in conjunction with the phrase *notes égales*, which suggests that *couler* cannot imply inequality.
These points are much disputed, but the weight of evidence is incontrovertibly against reverse inequality, i.e., short-long patterns.

3. POINTER or PIQUER (very crisp over-dotting)

In the context of a passage of quavers normally played *louré*

a dotted note(s) should be interpreted as though it were double-dotted:

A concluding comment from Engramelle: 'inequalities . . . in many places vary in the same piece; it is left to fine taste to appreciate these variations of inequality . . . a little more or less inequality substantially changes the expression of a piece.'[5]

The more common ornaments

Many composers left tables of ornaments together with details of their execution. A close study of these reveals certain anomalies, and in order to avoid confusion, the ornaments listed below are those most commonly found in the organ repertoire of *le grand siècle*, together with their most usual realizations.

The *port de voix* (appoggiatura), as indicated by its name, had vocal origins; its most usual purpose being a one-note grace (or ornament) ascending or gliding upwards to the main note (for explanation, see page 139), causing an accented dissonance resolving onto a consonance.

 with the first quaver stressed (slightly lengthened).

It is alternatively indicated as follows:  or

It is also found descending:  or or

being played  again with stress on the first qua

Sometimes the *port de voix* is found with a lombardic rhythm

and with greater leaps or intervals

 played

The *port de voix* is often linked with the *pincé* (mordent), which lat ornament on its own was usually interpreted as follows:

and = or depending on the

The two together being indicated thus:

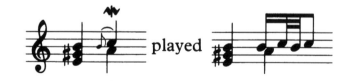 played

with stress on the first semiquave

[5] Donington, p.452

...he *cadence* (turn)

is usually interpreted:

...hen placed immediately above a note, or when placed between:

interpreted

...should not be confused with the sign for the *pincé* (see above).

...he *pincé* was sometimes extended to the *pincé double* (double ...ordent), with no special sign of its own

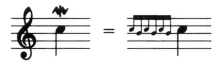

...e *tremblement* (trill) is sometimes confusingly known as *cadence* ...d has several slightly different forms; the simple form being:

...B. this ornament commences on the upper auxiliary]

...is sometimes found in combination with the *pincé* known as the ...emblement et pincé:

and at other times, together with the *port de voix*

also in combination with the *cadence:*

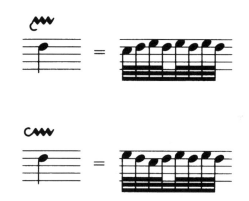

In his treatise *L'art de toucher le clavecin*, 1716, Couperin described the make-up of the *tremblement* as follows:

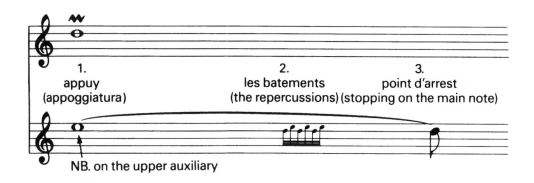

| 1. appuy (appoggiatura) | 2. les batements (the repercussions) | 3. point d'arrest (stopping on the main note) |

NB. on the upper auxiliary

He continues: 'Other trills are arbitrary; some have an *appoggiatura*, and others are so short that they have neither *appoggiatura* nor do they linger on the last note'.

The *coulé* seems to have many different forms, but the two most commonly met with are as follows:

i)

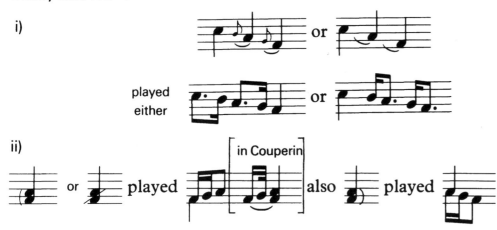

ii) above is alternatively known as *Tierce coulé.*

The *slide* is easier to understand:

usually the two grace-notes taking time from the previous note:

or, occasionally from the final note:

alternatively known as *port-de-voix double.*

The *Arpègement* (arpeggio)

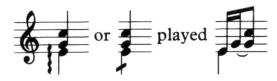

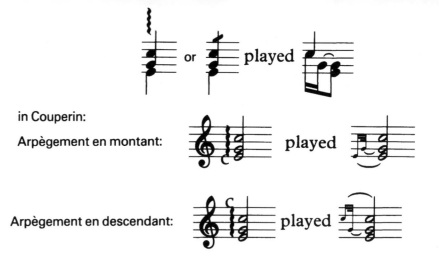

in Couperin:

Arpègement en montant: played

Arpègement en descendant: played

The manner of playing

Several composers left instructions as to how certain movements shou be played. Those of André Raison from the preface to his first *Liv d'Orgue* (1688) are given here because they are perhaps the most succin He heads it

'HOW GRACE AND MELODIC CHARM ARE GIVEN TO ALL THESE PIECES'

A GRAND PLEIN JEU is played very slowly. The chords should be quite legato one to the other, taking pains not to raise one finger until the other has pressed down; and the last measure should be much prolonged.
The PETIT PLEIN JEU is played lightly and fluently.

The DUO, a free and easy style of piece, is played rapidly and pointedly when written in quavers.

The RECIT DE CROMORNE, or DE TIERCE is played very tenderly. Accentuate cadences in important keys, particularly the last one.

The CORNET is played with celerity, animation, and fluidity; and the chief cadences should be lengthened, especially the last.

The BASSE DE TROMPETTE, CROMORNE, and TIERCE are played boldly and neatly, with vitality and spark.

The CROMORNE EN TAILLE is played very tenderly.

The TIERCE EN TAILLE is played straightforwardly and fluently.

The VOIX HUMAINE is played compassionately and very legato.

The DIALOGUE on two, three, and four manuals is played according to the indicated tempo.

He also implies that in organ music found to have some relation to t dance (much of it has!), it should be played like a dance, but a little slow because of the sanctity of the church.

Dotted notes: Assuming that the quavers in the following extract from orrette's *Cromhorne en Taille* are played *inégales*, it would be customary play those quavers following the dotted notes in the same manner.

heavily punctuated, dotted, overture-type pieces, the following

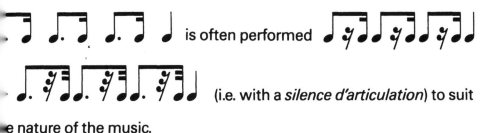

is often performed (i.e. with a *silence d'articulation*) to suit e nature of the music.

But  is normally slurred implying <u>no</u> *silence d'articulation* at the dot.

At cadential trills with dotted notes

the interpretation should probably be

and at cadences without ornament signs, but with a cadential trill implied

the intepretation should probably be (approximately)

It is important to note that all short notes in trill notation serve as an indication of the notes to be played. The value of the note is only approximate. They should generally gather momentum during their course.

Some contrasting pieces follow by Michel Corrette and Louis Marchand. Realizations of the ornaments may be found under **The more common ornaments** earlier in this Chapter, p.156.

3 movements from the Magnificat on the 3rd and 4th tones from *Premier Livre d'Orgue*, 1737
Plein jeu avec la Pedalle de Trompette pour toucher avec les deux pieds ('Plein jeu' with the Pedal Trumpet (8') for both feet)*

[Corrette lists the stops as follows: *G.O.* Bourdon 16', Montre [8'], Bourdon [8'], Prestant [4'], Doublette [2'], Fourniture, and Cymballe. POS to G.O. *POS:* Bourdon [8'], Montre [8'], Prestant [4'], Doublette [2'], Fourniture, and Cymballe. He also states that 'Adagio means very slowly'.]

Michel Corrette (1709-95)

Pedalle de Trompette

*The double pedal part should be played with the toes only, and a *détaché* touch. If the student finds this piece too difficult to master, it is advisable to miss it out and move on to the next one.

Récit de Nazard

[Corrette's registrations: *G.O.:* Bourdon [8′] and Prestant [4′] or Montre [8′] . *POS:* Bourdon [8′] , Prestant [4′] and Nazar [2⅔′] . He states that 'Largo means slowly, with taste'.]

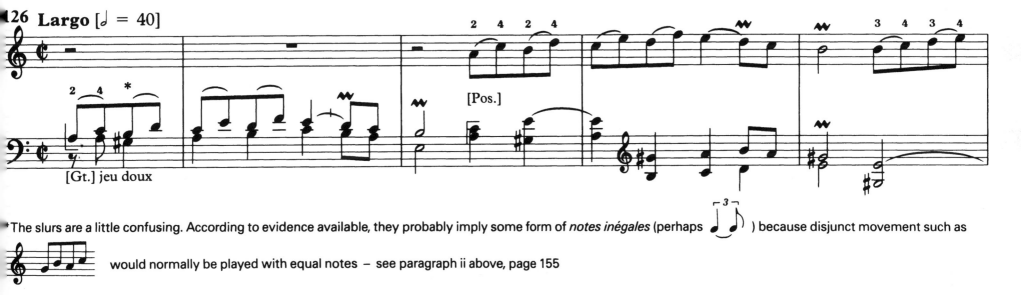

*The slurs are a little confusing. According to evidence available, they probably imply some form of *notes inégales* (perhaps ♩♪) because disjunct movement such as

would normally be played with equal notes – see paragraph ii above, page 155

Cromhorne en Taille

G.O.: Bourdon 16', Bourdon [8'] , Prestant [4'] . *POS:* Cromhorne [8'] , Bourdon [8'] , Prestant [4'] . Pedalles de Flûtes [16' and 8']*

A mild lilting *inégalité* would be appropriate throughout [see pages 154-5].

127 **Adagio** [♩ = 60]

[Gt.] jeu doux

[Pos.] Cromhorne

Pedalles de flûtes

*Corrette gives no pitches for the Flûtes. In view of the fact that the 16' Bourdon is used in the G.O. the implication is that a matching 16' Bourdon was available to him in the Pedal, or that he would have expected the Tirasse G.O. (Gt. to Ped. coupler) to have been drawn. The more common pedal registration is 'Pédalles de Flûte', meaning Flûte 8' alone. In view of the short pedal keys and the fact that they slanted downwards towards the player, an all-toes technique and *détaché* touch would seem appropriate. (See *L'Art du Facteur d'Orgues* by Dom Bedos de Celles, plate 52).

- pieces

Tierce en taille from *Première suite de pièces d'orgue* (1700).

Marchand does not appear to have left written comments as to how his works should be performed, but Gaspard Corrette (father of Michel) published his 'Mass on the 8th tone' in 1703, and wrote 'The "Tierce en taille" demands languidness and nuance, then sweeping passages, full of movement'. (from *The Language of the Classical French Organ* by Fenner Douglass, p.196)

[see pages 152-4 for registration suggestions]

Louis Marchand (1669-1732/3)

The second semiquaver of this bar should perhaps be 1 tone lower (*a*).

Basse de Trompette (ou de Cromhorne)
[see pages 152-3 for registration suggestions]

*This movement is probably too fast, and the 'Basse' too disjunct, for it to be played *inégale*. A *détaché* touch throughout is recommended. Gaspard Corrette wrote, in 1703, of the 'Basse de Trompette' that 'it is performed daringly, imitating a fanfare'. (Fenner Douglass, p.196).

Fond d'orgue*

[see pages 153-4 for registration suggestions]

*The quavers in this piece could be *inégales*. Gaspard Corrette writes (1703) that 'The "Fond d'orgue" must be played tenderly, in a "cantabile style". (Fenner Douglass, p.196). Additional ornamentation would enhance the expressive nature of the piece.

Dialogue†
[see pages 153-4 for registration suggestions]

†Gaspard Corrette writes (1703) 'The "Dialogue" is played very boldly, ranging among all sorts of moods, from gaiety to languor.' (Fenner Douglass, p.196).
*The pedals were probably not intended to be used until ★
**From this point a *détaché* touch with mildly lilting quavers can be effective.

It is possible that the pedals were used *en ravalement* for these notes (i.e. reinforcing the manual notes at the octave below on the REED STOPS)

**It can be effective to make a slight *ritard.* towards the end of each 'Echo' section.

5 Further points about articulation and fingering

From points raised in Chapter 1, it is fairly safe to assume that organ-playing in and around the time of J.S. Bach was less *legato* than might have been imagined by more recent performers (1850-1950). Indeed, *legato* as we know it today would have been impossible in some passages without resorting to changing fingers on held notes, known as **finger substitution**.

FINGER SUBSTITUTION

As mentioned in Chapter 1, only one piece has survived with fingerings by J.S. Bach himself (Applicatio, BWV 994, page 21). There are other pieces in which the fingering may be by Bach, or inspired by his teaching. These are Praeludium in G minor (BWV 930) and Praeludium (Chapter 1, page 33) and Fughetta in C (BWV 870a). In all of these there is only one instance of finger substitution. The evidence seems to be that it was not customarily practised in early music, with the exception of Couperin, who makes mention of it in *L'art de toucher le clavecin*, 1716. One of the reasons for its limited use could have been that the natural keys were shorter than those normally met with in romantic and modern organs. There simply would not have been enough room on the keyboard for much finger substitution!

A marked contrast is apparent between the different keyboard Tutors through the ages. A gradual shift from *détaché* touch to *legato* can be traced through the writings of Couperin, Clementi, Lemmens, Stainer, Vierne, Dupré, Videro and others. Nicholas Jacques Lemmens (1823-81) is said to have brought about a revolution in organ-playing (his *Ecole d'orgue* was published in 1862), not only by his development of pedal technique, but by introducing finger substitution, a technical accomplishment indispensible to *legato* playing. [1]

Finger substitution gradually becomes more thoroughly taught, and even *glissando* is a subject taken seriously. Louis Vierne (1870-1937) is at pains to teach substitution at the easiest level, and moves step by step through to quite complicated manoeuvres, indicating how he would have wished his own music to be performed with a good *legato* touch.

In these exercises for both finger substitution and *glissando*, the student should try to achieve a touch in which no gap is audible between the notes played. It should not be possible to hear the starting transient of the pipes.

[1] Léon Vallas, *César Franck*, p.104, Harrap

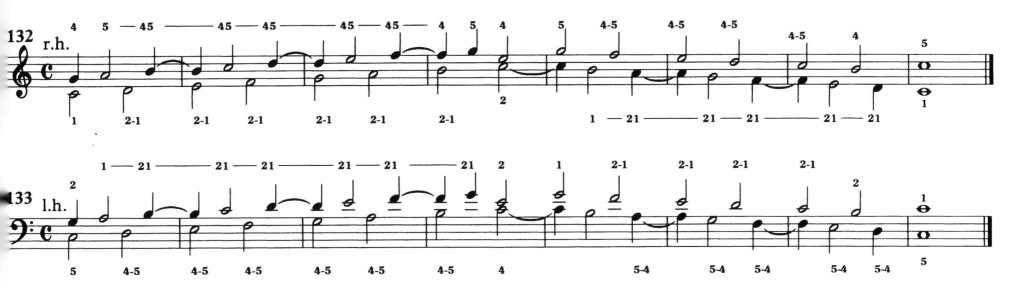

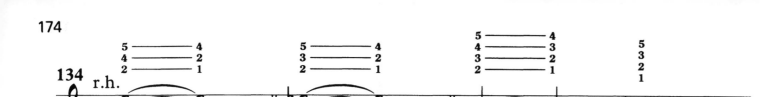

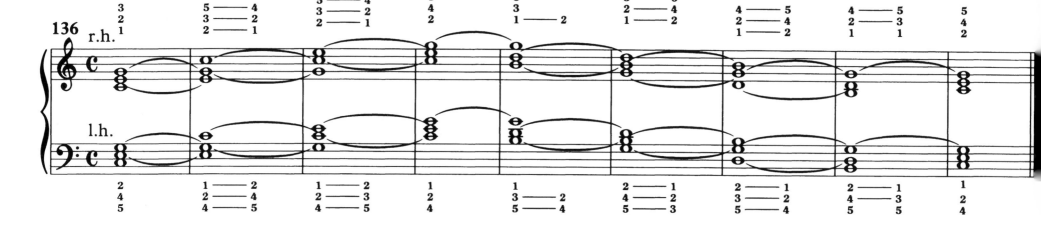

Similarly, in demonstrating his desire for complete *legato*, Marcel Dupré (1886-1971) fingered and footed every note in many of his editions. It should be said, however, that he, together with Flor Peeters, Finn Videro and others, was keen on repeated notes being treated in the following way:

and he often wrote a *staccato* dot over the note indicating that it should be played for half its value. This is an admirable way to ensure clarity in part-playing and in melodic lines where repeated notes occur. The result, however, is quite different from the Baroque *ordinary procedure* (touch) – see Chapter 1, under *Touch*. It can be an advantage to employ alternating fingers on repeated notes where possible (as in the example by Scheidt in Chapter 1) in order to gain clarity and articulation.

GLISSANDO (i.e. sliding):

Joseph Bonnet (1884-1944) in his edition of the *Trois Chorals* of César Franck writes (in 1942): 'Intelligent phrasing, smooth and singing style, and a perfect *legato* are required. But there can be no real *legato* when the same finger moves from one key to another, except when it slides carefully from a black key to the next white one. This is true, not only in playing the outer parts of the polyphony (soprano and bass) but also in playing the inner voices (alto and tenor). In order to achieve a perfect and clean *legato*, which of course should never be confused with muddy playing, we are obliged to use very careful fingerings: substitutions of fingers on the same note when necessary, or changing from one hand to another. In many cases we have to use still other means. One of the most important of these enables the thumb to do the work of two fingers: first, the wrist being kept in a low position, we touch a white key with the thumb's phalanx, with the tip of the thumb positioned over the next white key to be played; second, by lifting the wrist slightly, the second note is played with the thumb's tip.'

Here are some exercises by Lemmens in order to become familiar with this technique. Practise very slowly counting 1-2, 1-2 for each quaver, making the changes from phalanx to tip as you count:

(in terms of the thumb, p = phalanx, t = tip)

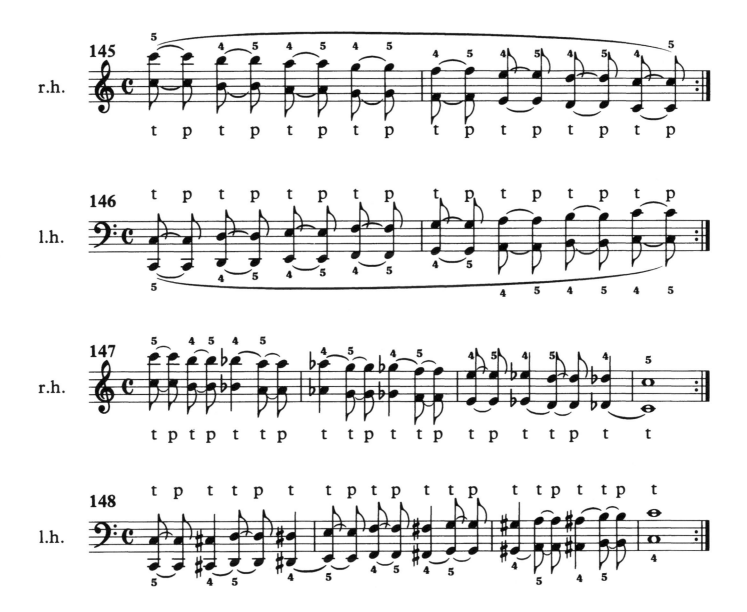

The different though closely related arts of touch, articulation, fingering (both early and more recent forms), and finger substitution, together with their parallels in the pedal department (including all-toes and toes-and-heels techniques) are necessary points of study for the organ student. It cannot be stressed enough how important they are. They are also difficult and require years of careful study – even the study of a lifetime!

6 Playing Hymns

Hymn-playing is a grossly underestimated art. A member of a congregation will assume that if you play the organ you automatically play hymns, and at any suitable pitch! Much careful training and practice is required to play them competently and at a reasonable pace for congregational singing.

USING THE PEDALS IN HYMNS

It is inadvisable to use the pedals in hymns during church services until a reasonable mastery of pedal-playing is achieved. There is nothing more distracting than frequent mistakes in the pedal-line. When practising hymn-playing, it is important to keep the pedal-line to the Bass part, while the left hand maintains its independence by playing the tenor part. Take one of the easiest hymns ever written as a starting point. Play the pedal line through using the suggested pedalling. Then add the left-hand part, making certain that the pedalling is adhered to. The left hand part may become easier if a little fingering is inserted.

First strain of Song 46, Orlando Gibbons (1583-1625)

Now try everything together, following the suggested markings carefully. Ensure that you choose a very slow tempo, and play with a good *legato*, taking care to articulate repeated notes:

In the early stages, it is important to go through this routine with every hymn you attempt. A hymn book will contain all the material you need. Choose hymns carefully in the beginning, avoiding complicated key signatures and textures. Never allow the left hand to play the bass part and avoid playing the pedal-line an octave below the given pitch. Keep practising the skill of independence by allowing the left hand to play the tenor part only. One further example is given here:

Ach Gott und Herr. Melody in *Neu-Leipziger-Gesangbuch*, 1682.

Adapted and harmonised by J. S. Bach

THE PLAY-OVER

On the Continent of Europe a *vorspiele* acts as an introduction. This usually takes the form of an improvised prelude based on the hymn to be sung. In Britain, however, the play-over or introduction is generally only the first half of the tune. There are exceptions to this, e.g. in the case of a long hymn, where only the first (and last) lines are sufficient to remind the congregation of the tune, or in cases where the central cadence is in a distant key, which might cause confusion over the starting note for the congregational first verse.

Ensure that the play-over is at precisely the tempo you require the congregation to sing. When the congregation joins in, maintain the tempo, even if it sounds to you as if you are leaving them behind. They'll soon catch up!

REGISTRATION

The play-over is often effective if played on a softer sound than verse one. Consider leaving out the pedals occasionally until the congregation joins in. The melody may be soloed out in the play-over (see below). See that your choice of REGISTRATION reflects the essence of the hymn's words. It can be distracting for a congregation to be singing Lenten words to Easter REGISTRATIONS! To avoid over-fussy REGISTRATION, keep the same one for a complete verse (if the words allow it) and change between each verse to an appropriate colour, thus enhancing the meaning of the text. Always allow adequate time for the congregation to breathe at the end of each line, except where the punctuation demands continuity. Watch out for the occasional comma during the course of a line, and allow time for a breath, if appropriate.

SOLO-ING OUT THE MELODY

Quite a useful technique is to be able to solo out the melody of a hymn-tune, and for this the left hand should play both tenor and alto parts. The right hand is then free to play the soprano melody on a SOLO STOP on another keyboard. The pedals should continue to play the bass:

Tallis' Canon

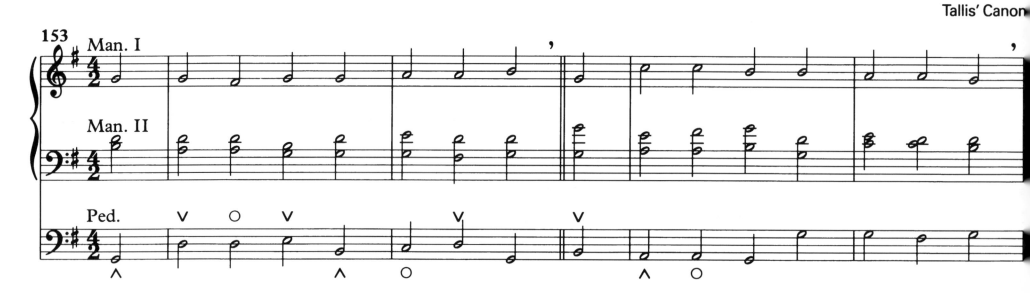

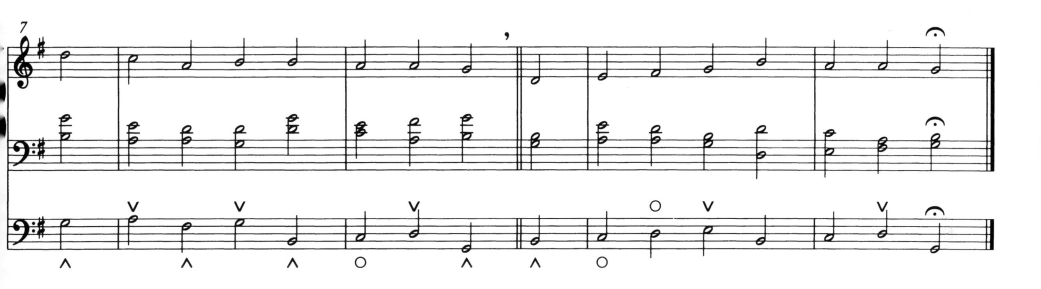

TRANSPOSITION

Congregations and choirs frequently request a higher or lower pitch in hymn-singing. It is sensible to commence the study of transposition as soon as hymn-playing is fluent, especially since it is included in many examination syllabuses. Here are some hints which may prove useful:

1. Think clearly of the new KEY before commencing.

2. Make sure you play the bass-line accurately throughout.

3. Briefly scan the hymn beforehand, establishing the direction of the KEY changes (e.g. relative minor or dominant), and thinking through the cadence points.

4. Look at the change of system, and memorize the first chord of the new system.

5. Hold on to any common notes there may be from one chord to the next – they are the transposer's free gift!

6. Learn the art slowly, carefully and rhythmically, and commence with the simplest hymn you can find.

7 Using the swell-pedal and the registration aids

THE SWELL PEDAL

SWELL pedals vary in style, design and positioning. The two most frequently met with are:

i) the ratchet SWELL-pedal, positioned towards the right-hand end of the PEDALBOARD, and therefore for the right foot:

ii) the balanced SWELL, positioned centrally, immediately above the pedals, though usually worked by the right foot:

When the right foot is not operating the pedal, the lever stays up (box closed), or it can be fixed down (box open). Sometimes there is a half-way position (box half open). Care must be taken to locate the 'notch' to avoid the swell box shutters closing with a bang! Remember that the first small opening of the shutters results in a much greater *crescendo* than can be obtained from all the remaining available movement.

he advantage with the balanced pedal is that it may be moved to any
esired position, and it will stay there when the foot is removed. Again,
ne initial opening should be carefully managed.

With both types it is necessary to be able to use them for the gradual
rescendo and diminuendo, and for the sforzando (the Italian term –

shortened form **sf** – denoting that a note or chord should be
emphasized). As the latter is comparatively rare, we will just deal with
the gradual technique. Here is a piece which can be played with hands
and (mainly) left foot together, while using the swell-pedal with the right
foot. Place the toe on the pedal in the case of the ratchet swell, and the
entire foot in the case of the balanced swell for optimum control.

viously, if a gradual crescendo or diminuendo is required by the
mposer, the pedalling used for that passage should be carefully
ranged to leave the right foot free to manipulate the SWELL-pedal or
ver.

EGISTRATION AIDS

ntinuing with the three playing traditions mentioned in chapter 4, it
mportant to know the facilities for changing REGISTRATION during the
urse of a movement which were available to composers. An under-
anding as to how they function is necessary in the study of the
ertoire.

In Britain, it would appear that the 'shifting action' was the only device
ailable to the organist in assisting with the REGISTRATION until the early
00s. It was certainly not fitted to every organ, but it is thought to have

dated from before the Commonwealth [1], although it is now virtually
obsolete. It was activated by a lever for the foot which had the effect of
shutting off part of the organ without necessarily moving the STOP knobs.
Usually, it was the UPPERWORK which was silenced, including the REEDS,
where these existed.

Mechanical COMPOSITION or COMBINATION PEDALS with fixed
combinations began to appear in the early 1800s (the invention of J.C.
Bishop [2]) and by the Great Exhibition of 1851 Willis had used the first
Thumb PISTONS [3]. Adjustable PISTONS, although in the beginning

[1] C.F. Abdy Williams, *The Story of the Organ*, Walter Scott (1916)
[2] William Leslie Sumner, *The Organ*, p.359
[3] Ibid, p.360

adjustable only by the organ tuner, began to appear from 1854[4], but the capture system did not come into common usage until the early 1900s. This was the system in which the organist could draw some STOPS by hand, and by pressing a 'setter' button, could store the COMBINATION into the desired piston by pneumatic, electro-pneumatic or electro-mechanical means.

More recently, computer technology has prompted the development of the solid-state piston system, in which enormous numbers of combinations may be stored. A sequencer is sometimes found, which will enable hundreds of different combinations to be memorized and brought into play in the required order at the pressure of the same thumb piston or toe lever. It is even possible to record these on a 'star card'. Each regular user of the organ may have his own card containing all his pre-selected COMBINATIONS, which he brings to the organ and takes with him when he finishes playing.

The revival of interest in early principles and design of organs is sometimes carried to the lengths in which new organs are built with no REGISTRATION aids at all.

Naturally, the most modern systems of REGISTRATION carry with them enormous flexibility, both from the point of view of control and of enabling a great mélange of organ colours and effects. But from studying the more restricted REGISTRATION aids of the late Victorian and Edwardian organ, it is possible to establish how the music of S.S. Wesley, Stanford, Parry or Elgar might have been performed. COMBINATIONS were not by any means standard, but the average 2-MANUAL organ may have been set up along the lines following this hypothetical SPECIFICATION:[5]

[4] Ibid, p.360

[5] Organs of this period often had a small Choir organ, too, comprising stops along the following lines: Hohl Flute 8′, Gamba 8′, Dulciana 8′, Flauto Traverso 4′, Corno di Bassetto 8′.

GREAT

Bourdon	16′
Open Diapason no. 1	8′
Open Diapason no. 2	8′
Hohl Flute	8′
Dulciana	8′
Principal	4′
Harmonic Flute	4′
Twelfth	2⅔′
Fifteenth	2′
Mixture	4 ranks
Trumpet	8′

SWELL

Bourdon	16′
Open Diapason	8′
Lieblich Gedact	8′
Gamba	8′
Voix Celeste TC	8′
Gemshorn	4′
Piccolo	2′
Mixture	3 ranks
Contra Oboe	16′
Cornopean	8′
Oboe	8′
Clarion	4′

PEDAL

Open Diapason	16′
Violone	16′
Bourdon	16′
Octave	8′
Bass Flute	8′
Trombone	16′
Trumpet	8′

The Great and Pedal COMBINATIONS often function in tandem, e.g. Gt. causes Ped. 1 to function in order to provide a balancing REGISTRATION. Sometimes a stop labelled 'Gt. & Ped. combs cpld' is available.

	GREAT		PEDAL		SWELL	
Combination 1:	Hohl Flute	8′	Bourdon	16′	Gamba	8′
	Dulciana	8′			Voix Celeste TC	8′
Combination 2:	Open Diapason no.2	8′	Bourdon	16′	Open Diapason	8′
	Hohl Flute	8′	Bass Flute	8′	Lieblich Gedact	8′
	Dulciana	8′			Gamba	8′
	Harmonic Flute	4′				
Combination 3:	Open Diapasons 1 & 2	8′	Violone	16′	Open Diapason	8′
	Hohl Flute	8′	Bourdon	16′	Lieblich Gedact	8′
	Dulciana	8′	Bass Flute	8′	Gamba	8′
	Octave	4′			Gemshorn	4′
	Harmonic Flute	4′				
Combination 4:	Bourdon	16′	Open Diapason	16′	Bourdon	16′
	Open Diapasons 1 & 2	8′	Violone	16′	Open Diapason	8′
	Hohl Flute	8′	Bourdon	16′	Lieblich Gedact	8′
	Dulciana	8′	Bass Flute	8′	Gamba	8′
	Principal	4′			Gemshorn	4′
	Twelfth	2⅔′			Oboe	8′
	Fifteenth	2′				
Combination 5:	Bourdon	16′	Open Diapason	16′	Bourdon	16′
	Open Diapasons 1 & 2	8′	Violone	16′	Open Diapason	8′
	Hohl Flute	8′	Bourdon	16′	Lieblich Gedact	8′
	Dulciana	8′	Octave	8′	Gamba	8′
	Principal	4′	Bass Flute	8′	Gemshorn	4′
	Twelfth	2⅔′	Trombone	16′	Piccolo	2′
	Fifteenth	2′	Trumpet	8′	Mixture	3 ranks
	Mixture	4 ranks			Contra Oboe	16′
	Trumpet	8′			Cornopean	8′
					Clarion	4′

ere are some tentative general guidelines[6] for registering British organ music from c.1890 to c.1930:

Different families of STOPS (e.g., DIAPASONS, FLUTES, STRINGS) were freely mixed.

In the build-up to Full Organ, 4′ FLUES were not drawn until all, or most of (except the Celeste) the 8′ FLUES were drawn, and 4′ UTES were added before 4′ PRINCIPALS. Also, MANUAL FLUE Doubles (i.e., 16′) were introduced at a relatively early stage.

Full Organ meant everything except the Celeste, i.e., even Dulcianas, Salicionals etc. were included.

MIXTURES were thought of as a bridge between FLUES and REEDS and never or seldom heard without the latter. This is another way saying that MIXTURES were for the Full Organ only.

y using only the above combinations of stops when you attempt the following piece by John E. West:

Kindly supplied by Relf Clark. See also "The BIOS Column" by him in *Organists' Review*, December 1991, p.285.

Impromptu (Introductory Voluntary)

John E. West (1863-1929)

In **Germany,** many composers in the Baroque era and earlier probably accepted the idea of 'block' REGISTRATION (i.e. in which the STOPS are drawn and left unchanged during the course of a movement) as befitting the nature of the organ, and considered that over-fussy REGISTRATION changes detracted from the form and structure of a work — notably [and arguably!] in a Bach Prelude and Fugue. By contrast, more recent composers often required a very gradual *crescendo* during the course of a movement (e.g. Max Reger, 1873-1916) and the CONSOLE equipment available to them in their lifetime gives us some clue as to how they made such complex changes in dynamics. This equipment is usually known as 'CONSOLE ACCESSORIES', or 'REGISTRATION AIDS'.

In a Reger Fugue, for example, it is possible to make a *crescendo* from one stop alone through to the full organ by means of the ROLLSCHWELLER or WALZE, without drawing a single STOP by hand. This is a cylinder located in the vicinity of the SWELL pedals and operated by the feet. It requires lots of practice in operation by those unused to it. Such an even *crescendo* is very difficult to achieve on the British and French organs single-handedly, and therefore many organists justifiably make use of REGISTRATION assistants to pull STOPS for them.

It was the rebuilding of the Merseburg Cathedral organ by Friedrich Ladegast[7] in 1853 which was to influence the style of writing for the organ throughout Germany. He incorporated a device known as an *Echozug*, in which the Full Organ could be reduced to a *pianissimo*. Presumably it was a mechanical form of ROLLSCHWELLER (mentioned above) which only worked from *ff* to *pp*. This led to the development of lots of ingenious devices, enabling the German organist to achieve an enormous range of colours, the smoothest *crescendos* and *diminuendos*, and the most dramatic and sudden *pp* or *ff*. The use of all these aids and controls is exemplified in the works of Reger. This complete about-turn in the German organ took place within a period of 50 years, and was facilitated by the advent of pneumatic motors and electricity. The days of fully mechanical action with no playing aids at all were past, but fortunately only temporarily. The revival of old principles of organ-building is now fully apparent (Orgelbewegung), and it is important to regard the organs of Reger's lifetime as historic instruments along with the surviving organs of earlier centuries. Another important playing aid, the FREE COMBINATION, is described in the Glossary.

In this Chorale Prelude by Reger, *Jesu, meine Zuversicht*, opus 67, some of the playing aids mentioned above might have been used, in particular the ROLLSCHWELLER. Try to achieve the equivalent effect on a British organ!

Sumner, pp.248, 484

Jesus, meine Zuversicht.

Finger substitution (see Chapter 5, page 173) and exchanging of feet will be necessary in order to achieve a good *legato* and manipulate the swell-pedal

[The registration should probably be restricted to quiet 8' stops, on the Sw and Ch. (or Gt.). If it is possible to add stops discreetly for the first 2 bars of system 4 the 'quasi f' will be easier to realize.]

Langsam (*Slowly*) [♪ = 60]

Max Reger (1873-1916)

In **France,** the renowned 19th-century organ-builder, Aristide Cavaillé-Coll, played an important part in the development of REGISTRATION aids, which were completely lacking before his time. Since the 1850s, his system of VENTIL pedals provided the accepted way in which French organists made *crescendos* and *diminuendos*. The organ which inspired César Franck the most was clearly the Cavaillé-Coll at Ste. Clotilde in Paris (1859), where he presided as organist from 1858 till his death in 1890. As Franck towered above all other composers of organ music of his generation, it follows that a study of the organ he played, and the way in which he would have managed the REGISTRATION, will lead to a greater understanding of the interpretation of French Romantic organ music.

It is difficult to be completely certain of the exact SPECIFICATION of this organ as it was known to Franck, because there is a lack of documentation from that time[8]. However, printed below is the probable SPECIFICATION and STOP-layout during Franck's lifetime:

Stops on the left side of console

Récit (upper manual)

				Ventil chests		
Voix Humaine	Voix Céleste	Viole de Gambe		*Flûte Octaviante*	*Trompette*	
8'	8'	8'		4'	8'	

Positif (middle manual)

Montre	Flûte Harmonique	Gambe	Bourdon	*Quinte*	*Plein Jeu*	*Cromorne/ Clarinette*
8'	8'	8'	8'	3'		8'

Grand-Orgue (lower manual)

Montre de 16p	Viole de Gambe	Bourdon	Prestant	*Quinte*	*Plein jeu harmonique*	*Trompette*
16'	8'	16'	4'	3'		8'

Pédale

	Contre-basse	Octave		*Bombarde*	*Trompette*	
	16'	4'		16'	8'	

Stops on the right side

Récit

(Sonnette)	*Clairon*		*Ventil chests* *Octavin*		Flûte harmonique	Bourdon	Basson-hautbois
	4'		2'		8'	8'	8'

Positif

Clairon		Trompette	Doublette	Flûte Octaviante	Prestant	Bourdon	Salicional/ Unda Maris
4'		8'	2'	4'	4'	16'	8'

Grand-Orgue

Clairon		Bombarde	Doublette	Octave	Flûte harmonique	Bourdon	Montre
4'		16'	2'	4'	4'	8'	8'

Pédale

	Clairon	Basson		Flûte/ Basse	Quintaton/ Soubasse
	4'	16'		8'	32'

---

[8] see *Toward an Authentic Interpretation of the Organ Works of César Franck*, Rollin Smith (Juilliard Performance Guide no.1), Pendragon Press.

Those registers in italics were activated by Cavaillé-Coll's VENTIL pedals, looking similar to our Victorian-style composition pedals placed just above the PEDALBOARD and operated by the feet. These VENTILS, together with pedal and MANUAL COUPLERS and various other devices, were known as *Pédales de combinaison.* This is how they were arranged at Ste. Clotilde:

Tirasses		Anches	Octaves graves			Anches			Accouplements		Tremolo	lever swell-pedal
G.O.	POS	Péd	G.O.	POS	RÉC/POS	G.O.	POS	RÉC	POS/G.O.	RÉC/POS		

Those italicized STOPS could be shut off or brought into play, severally or collectively, by the VENTIL pedals which generally numbered one per department and were known under the heading *appels des anches* (literally 'call of the REEDS'). As an example, when we find the direction *Ajoutez les Anches du Grand Orgue* (add the REEDS of the GREAT organ), we may assume that all or some of those italicized STOPS on the GREAT will already have been drawn before commencing to play, yet silenced by the VENTIL pedal in readiness to be added en bloc as directed. Thus, it may be seen that a fairly large number of STOPS may be brought on or silenced in one movement of the foot without causing a single drawstop to move.

At Ste. Clotilde only four VENTIL pedals were needed to make a *crescendo* from the foundations (Les Fonds) to the full organ (Grand Choeur) – *Anches Récit, Anches Positif, Anches Grand-orgue* and *Anches Pédale,* all or some of the STOPS in italics having been pre-selected. In addition to these, unison and SUB-OCTAVE COUPLERS could be added, also by the feet. It should be noted that the Hautbois 8' of the Récit (the SWELL Oboe 8') is not activated by the VENTIL, but is considered one of the foundations of the SWELL. It can therefore be assumed that when the direction *Ôtez les Anches du Récit* (take off the REEDS of the SWELL) appears in the score, the Hautbois, also a REED of course, will still remain in play. In making a *crescendo* or *diminuendo* it will be observed that REGISTRATION changes could be made without lifting the hands from the keys.

In the following piece by Samuel Rousseau, who was choirmaster for some years at Ste. Clotilde, much use is made of the VENTIL system of REGISTRATION, and it is advisable to refer to the above stop-list to see which STOPS were most likely to have been activated by the VENTILS. This work should serve as a guide as to how to register much of the French Romantic repertoire. On the Cavaillé-Coll instrument, one would naturally follow all the French MANUAL changes, and make use of the VENTILS and COUPLERS. However, the British CHOIR organ is generally not strong enough to act as French Positif, and where there is a Rückpositiv, it seldom contains the Foundation STOPS required. Therefore, the REGISTRATION suggestions in English follow a 2-MANUAL scheme, in which the GREAT serves as both Grand Orgue and Positif. Usually, the dynamic markings *p* and *f* refer to the use of the SWELL box, but in the case of the *f* and *ff* markings for the Grand Orgue, we should take it to mean that all the Foundations are used at *f,* with the addition of the VENTIL STOPS at *ff.*

Offertoire Funèbre

Samuel Rousseau (1853-1904)

Swell: [Open Diapason 8'] , Gedact 8', Gamba 8', Gemshorn 4', Piccolo 2', Cornopean 8', Clarion 4', Oboe 8'. *Great:* Bourdon 16', Open Diapasons 1 and 2, Hohl Flute 8', Dulciana 8', Principal 4', [Flute 4'] . *Pedal:* Bourdon 16', Bass Flute 8'. Sw. to Gt., Gt. to Ped., Sw. to Ped.

Gd. O. *f*

Pos.

p (Swell box closed)

Gd. O. *ff*

Pos. *p*

Play the Pos. passages on a reduced Gt. (Open No. 2, 8')

[Full Gt.]

Otez Tirasse
There is no need to remove Gt. to Ped. Simply reduce Gt

Récit.

Pos.

Otez les Anches du Récit.
Remove 4', 2', Cornopean and Clarion from Sw.
l.h. plays on Gt.

Récit

[both hands on Sw.]

Gt. to Ped. off
Sw. to Ped. off

Pos.

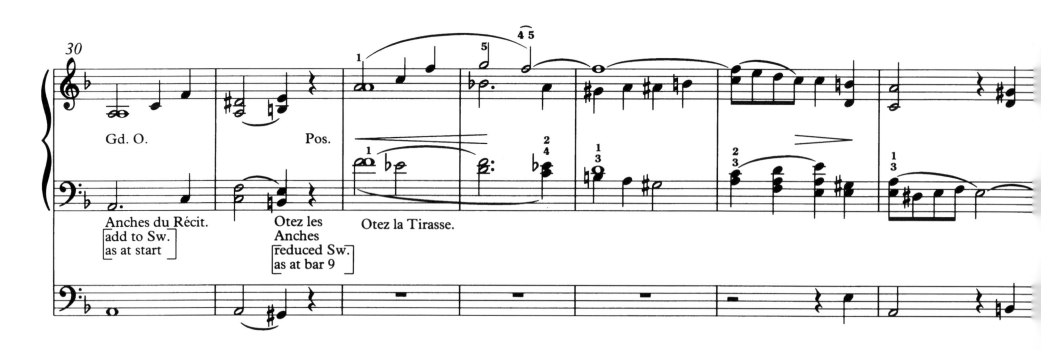

8 Beginning to improvise

Most organists at some stage in their career are expected to be able to improvise. In a church service the priest or minister will often ask for music to be played during part of the worship. This may take the form of an extempore addition to the offertory hymn, or it may involve simply filling in an otherwise awkward silence. Wherever these moments occur, it is important that the organist is prepared to improvise in a manner which is worthy of an act of worship, and that the art of improvisation is allotted some rehearsal time.

While not attempting in any way to be a full course in improvisation, the following should enable the student to gain confidence in the art. Improvising well is often the result of much diligent study, and hours of working with carefully contrived musical clichés within certain frameworks.

The most successful improvisations are those with some sort of structure or basic form. In the early stages, this could be along the following lines:

1. a) A set pattern of 2, 3 or 4 chords played repeatedly by the left hand and pedals, with an improvised melody for the right hand.

   b) A similar pattern of 2, 3 or 4 chords played repeatedly by the right hand and pedals, with a melody for the left hand.

2. Using a Cantus Firmus (e.g. a hymn-tune), and creating another part above or below it.

3. Variations on a Ground Bass.

Stick firmly to the idea you begin with. Don't meander! Choose chordal sequences which flow well.

1. Continue playing the left hand and pedal chords in sequence, and improvise a right hand part on a SOLO STOP, with a different rhythm from that of the chords. There is no need to use accidentals in the following exercises.

158

2. Try completing the left hand part*, first in crotchets alone, and then with some quaver movement.

And now with the melody in the left hand, with the right hand improvising at first a part in crotchets and then including some quavers.

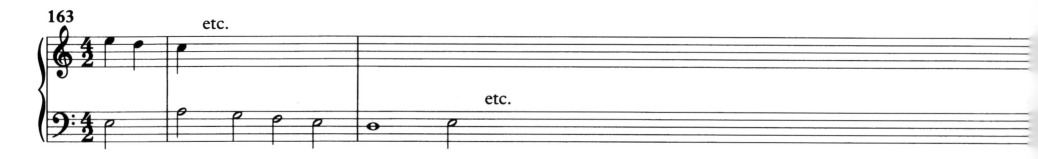

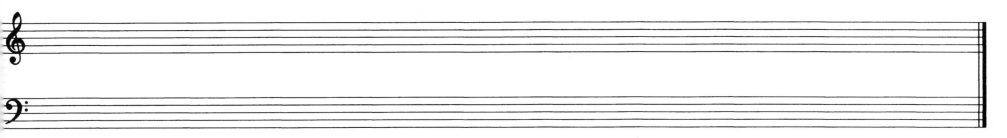

*To be avoided:

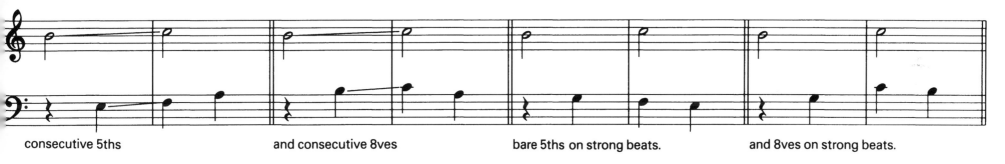

consecutive 5ths   and consecutive 8ves   bare 5ths on strong beats.   and 8ves on strong beats.

Variations on a Ground Bass.
Play this simple bass-line through several times, memorizing it.

Pedals:

Then work to the following formula, gradually increasing the contrapuntal movement.

a) Play over the theme on the pedals, and stick to the theme throughout – play each variant twice, with identical notes.
b) Addition of left hand part in similar note values (avoiding consecutive fifths and octaves – see below)*.
c) Addition of right hand part in similar note values (always avoiding consecutive fifths and octaves).
d) Introduce some crotchet movement to the right hand part and some in the left hand part.
e) Introduce the occasional dotted note.
f) Then, some quaver movement.
g) Finish with chords above the bass, ensuring good arrangement of parts, and possibly including some rests.

To be avoided:

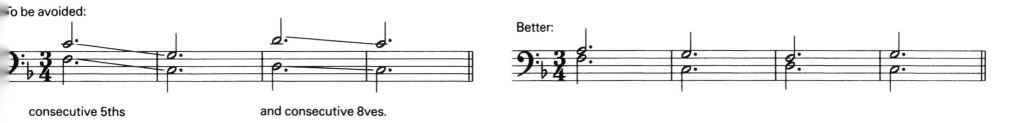

consecutive 5ths   and consecutive 8ves.   Better:

After having played this twice continue immediately to (b) and so on.

164

fine

ork with these bass-lines, following the same formula:

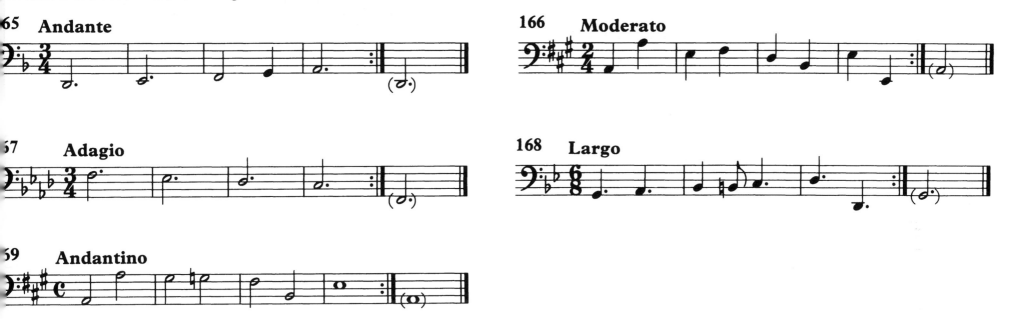

Further pieces to practise

he pieces in this chapter appear, for the most part, without fingering, pedalling and REGISTRATION suggestions, because it is expected that the student ll now be sufficiently competent to organize these matters personally, under the guidance of a teacher.

All pieces in this volume are suitable for use as Voluntaries in church services. Assuming that you are playing at a reasonable standard, you may sh to play at services, and a good way to begin is to become articled to an Organist and Choirmaster by becoming an Organ Scholar. Many churches w have scholarships available for organists wishing to gain experience. Make sure not to commit yourself to too much playing before you are ready. sensible way to begin is by preparing to play a hymn. Later, you could perhaps play a prelude voluntary. It may be some time before you are ready play for a whole service.

Care should be exercised in choosing appropriate music for the required time in the church calendar. As an obvious example, a Christmas musical eme would not be acceptable in Lent! Try to be sympathetic to the requirements of the liturgy. It can help the devotions of the congregation if voluntaries e related to the theme of the service, or are based on a hymn-tune(s) to be sung at the service. Familiarize yourself with the liturgical year, whichever nomination you play for, and ensure that what you play is fitting and inspiring.

Prelude in E flat

J. C. Kittel (1732-1809)

170 [Moderato] [♩ = 96]

*A REGISTRATION with an independent pedal is required. See in particular bar 31.

*Probably intended thus:

Vater unser im Himmelreich

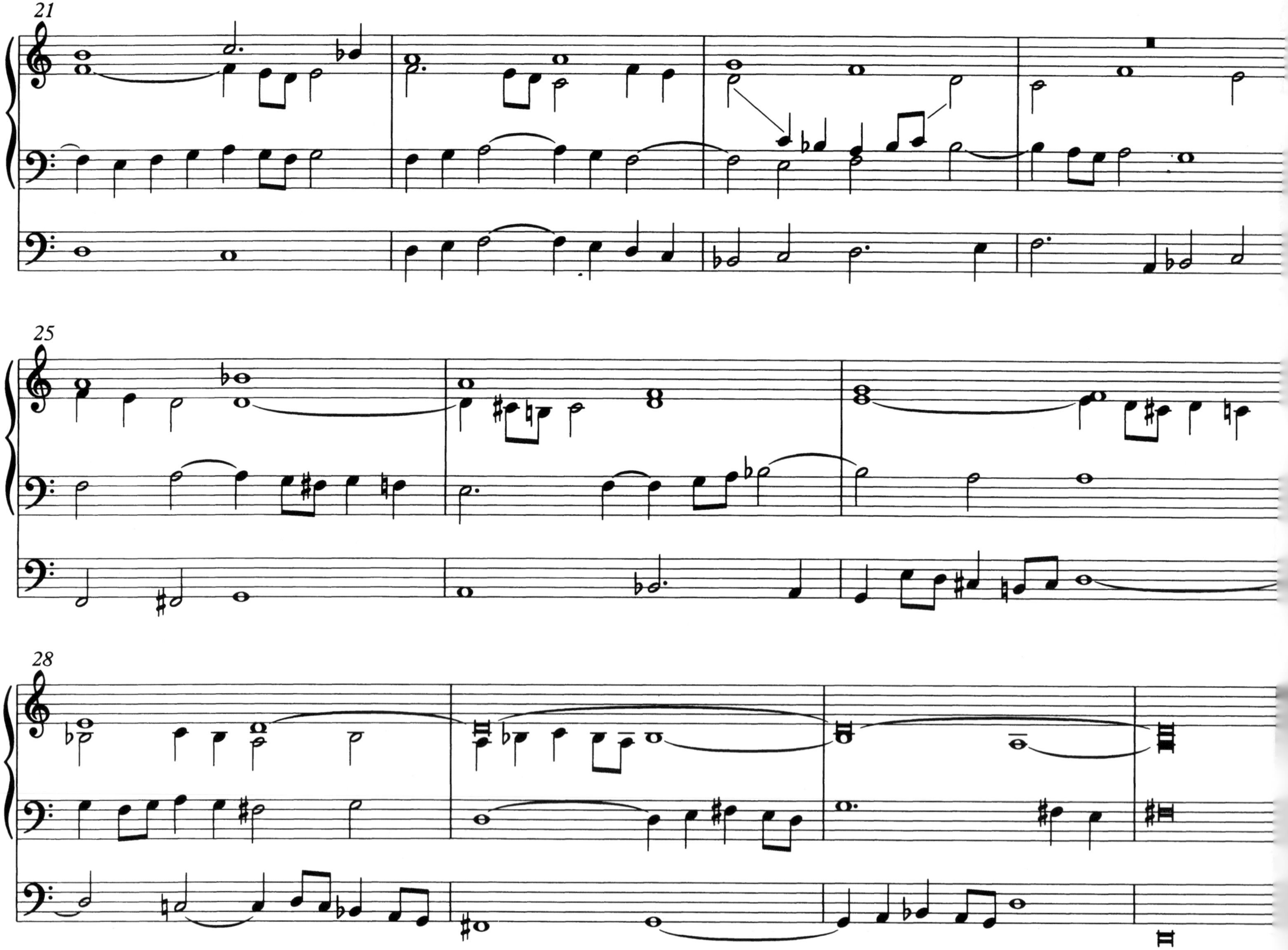
21
25
28

Vor deinen Thron tret' ich

This work is said to have been dictated from his death-bed, and may have been his last composition. For a full discussion, see *The Organ Music of J.S. Bach* by Peter Williams, Vol.II, p.170, Cambridge University Press.

[This Chorale Prelude sounds very well on simple registration, with both hands on the same keyboard. However, it is possible to 'solo out' the Chorale, if desired.]

172 [♩ = 44]

J. S. Bach, BWV 668

Herr Gott, dich loben alle wir, 2 Clav. and Pedal. In Canone all' Ottava

J. C. Oley (1738-89)

Allegro maestoso, Opus 15, no.7

Gustav Merkel (1827-85)

[♩ = 116]

Nun danket alle Gott, opus 135a, no.18

An exercise in adding STOPS from a *forte* dynamic level in order to finish on the full organ. The voices should all be played *legato* but the chorale melody in the top voice should be played a little *détaché* in order to stress it.

Max Reger (1873-1916)

Vom Himmel hoch, da komm ich her, opus 135a, no.24

An exercise in *legato* playing, use of SWELL-pedal, and subtle changes of STOPS to satisfy Reger's dynamics.

Max Reger

* NB. The Chorale melody transfers to the pedals at these points. Care should be taken to register the pedal line clearly.

An exercise in crisp, *détaché* and *legato* touches, with MANUAL or REGISTRATION changes (with PISTONS or COMBINATION PEDALS) in order to achieve the dynamics required. The pedals may be used on the notes indicated.

J. L. Battmann (19th century)

Vesper Voluntaries II and III

Edward Elgar (1857-1934)

179 **Andantino** [♩ = 80]

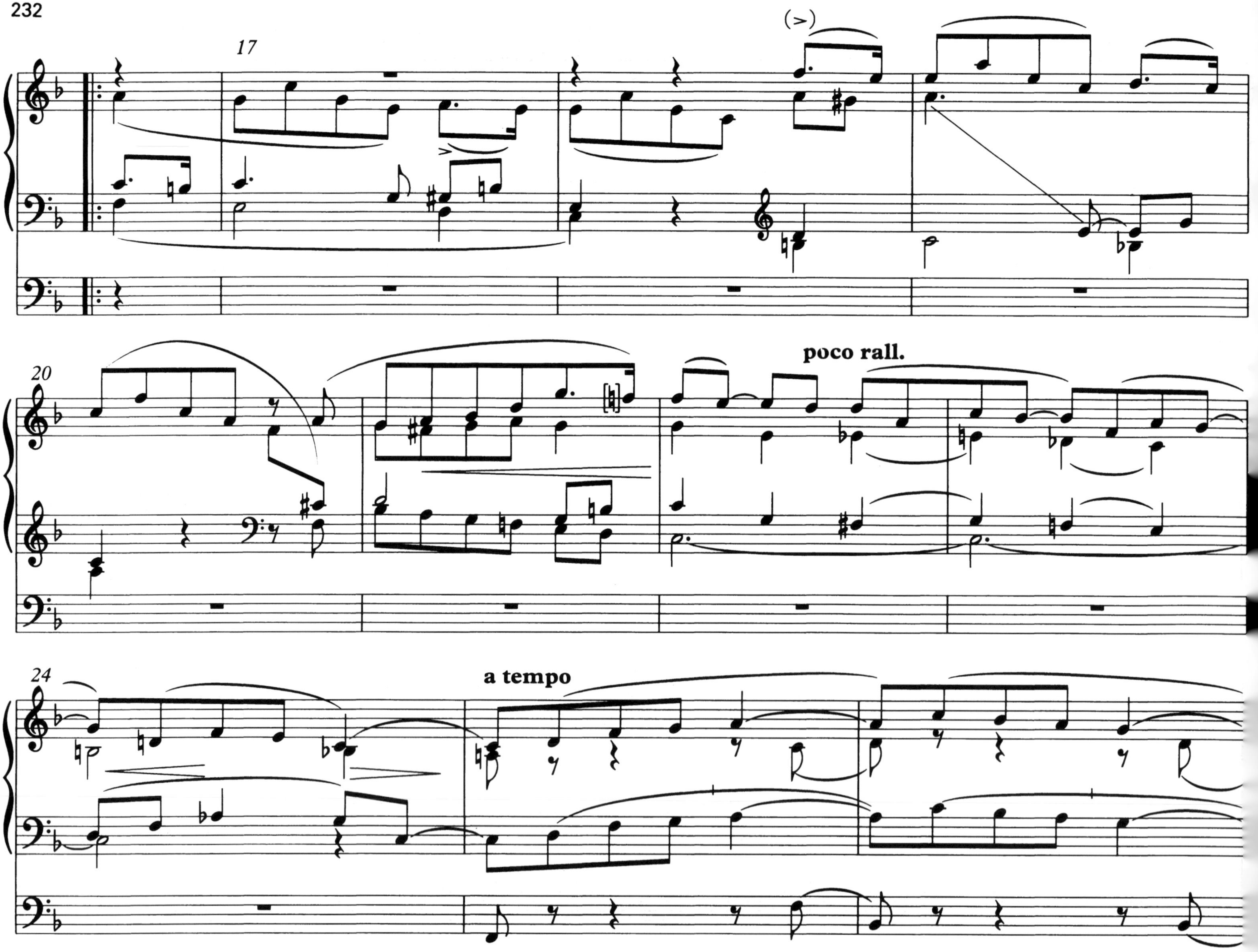
17
(>)
20
poco rall.
24
a tempo

Andante Sostenuto (No.2 from *Four Impressions*)

[Registration: *Swell:* soft 8′; *Great:* Flutes 8′ and 4′; *Choir:* Clarinet 8′; *Pedal:* soft 16′; Swell to Great, Swell to Pedal]

Guy H. Eldridge
1904 - 76

Andante sostenuto [♩ = 76]

Pastorale

Bryan Kelly
1934-

60
mp Gt. Flutes 8′, 4′
mp Sw. soft Reed, 4′ Principal, Larigot
p Sw. 8′ Salicional, 4′ Flute
Sw. to Ped. off
67
poco slentando.....
p
Gt.
16′, 8′ uncpld.
74
−4′
Sw. 8′, 2′

This work evokes the spirit of the Passion Chorale. The bass line is almost identical to one of the harmonizations of J.S. Bach.

[Registration: *Sw.* Quintadena 16′, Baarpÿp 8′ (a soft reed stop); *Gt.* Viola di Gamba 8′, Roerfluit 8′ (Rohrflute); *Ped.* Principaal 32′, Subbas 16′, Octaaf 8′ (Octave), Holfluit 8′; *Sw.* to *Gt.*]

Albert de Klerk
1917-

Delicato ♪ = 84

Preludietto (No.1 of *Four Short Pieces*)

[Registration: *Gt.* Full (without mixtures); *Sw.* Full; *Ped.* Full (without reeds); Gt. to Ped.]

Camil Van Hulse, Opus 94

183 **Robusto** ♩ = 100

[Nachspiel] No.149 from *Practical Organ School*, Part 3

J. C. H. Rinck (1770-1846)

*The author recommends omitting the upper pedal notes here to create a better texture.

10 Repertoire list

PIECES FOR FURTHER STUDY

The following is not intended to be a complete list, but to offer suggestions of pieces for further study. The publishers given are generally the recommended ones, although there may be other editions available unknown to the author.

FOR MANUALS ONLY:

Title of Volume/composer	Publisher/Editor

English Organ Music:
an anthology from four centuries in ten volumes — Novello/Langley
1. John Ambrose to John Bull
2. Orlando Gibbons to Matthew Locke
3. from John Blow to John Stanley
4. from Henry Purcell to John Stanley
5. from John Stanley to John Keeble
6. from John Keeble to Samuel Wesley (some with pedals)

Faber Early Organ Series, 18 Volumes — Faber/Dalton
European organ music of the 16th and 17th centuries
England:
1. c.1510-1590 Redford, Preston, Tallis, Blitheman, Byrd
2. 1590-1650 Byrd, Weelkes, O. Gibbons, Bull, Cosyn, Tomkins, etc.
3. 1660-1710 C. Gibbons, Locke, Blow, Purcell, Croft
Spain and Portugal:
4. c.1520-1620 Santa Maria, Bermudo, Cabezón, etc.
5. c.1620-c.1670 Correa de Arauxo, Aguilera de Heredia, etc.
6. c.1650-c.1710 Bruna, Martin y Coll collection, Cabanilles, etc.
France:
7. 1531-1660 Attaignant, Titelouze, Roberday, etc.

8. 1650-90 L. Couperin, d'Anglebert, Nivers, LeBègue, Raison, etc. (some with pedals)
9. 1690-1710 F. Couperin, Marchand, Guilain, deGrigny, Clérambault, etc. (some with pedals)
South Germany and Austria
13. 1512-77 Schlick, Hofhaimer, Kleber, Buchner, Schmid, etc.
14. c.1600-c.1660 Klemm, Kindermann, Froberger, etc.
Italy:
16. 1517-99 M. & G. Cavazzoni, A. Gabrieli, Merulo, etc.
17. c. 1600-35 Diruta, Trabaci, Banchieri, Frescobaldi, etc.

Tallis to Wesley series	Hinrichsen/Philips
An R.C.O. Miscellany	Basil Ramsey/ Johnstone
Anonymous:	
Voluntaries in A minor, G minor	Novello
Bennett J:	
Voluntaries 9 & 10	Novello/Johnstone
Boyce:	
10 Voluntaries	OUP
Camidge:	
Concerto no.2	Novello/Jackson
Clérambault:	
2 Suites	Kalmus
Cosyn:	
3 Voluntaries	Novello/Steele
Couperin:	
Pièces d'Orgue (2 Masses)	Oiseau-Lyre (UMP)
(some have pedals)	Kalmus
Croft:	
Organ Works	OUP/Platt
Daquin:	
Noëls (some have pedals)	Faber/Hogwood
Heron:	
10 Voluntaries (Incognita Organo 29)	Harmonia

Howells:
2 Pieces for Organ (manuals) — Novello
Nares:
6 Fugues with Introductory Voluntaries — OUP
Nielsen:
29 Short Preludes — Skandinaviska (Chester)

Pachelbel:
Fugues on the Magnificat — Novello
Pepusch:
Voluntary in C — OUP/Sanger
Pescetti:
Sonata in C minor — OUP/Hurford
Purcell:
Organ Works — Novello/McLean
Roberday:
Fugues & Caprices — Schott/Guilmant
Russell:
Voluntaries (2 vols.) — OUP/Langley
Complete Organ Works — Gillian Ward Russell
(some have pedals)
Stanley:
Voluntaries (in facsimile) — OUP
Sweelinck:
Organ Works (some have pedals) — Dover
Telemann:
Choralevorspiele (vol.1) — Bärenreiter
Kleine Fugen und Freie Orgelstücke (vol.2)
(some with pedals)
Wesley (S.)
12 short pieces — Hinrichsen

FOR MANUAL AND PEDALS:

Note: '(selected pieces)' or '(selected movements)' implies that these volumes contain some works which may be suitable for the student who has mastered the works in this Tutor. *Denotes volumes with exercises in trio-playing.

English Organ Music:
9. Thomas Attwood to Thomas Attwood Walmisley — Novello/Langley

Faber Early Organ Series, 18 volumes — Faber/Dalton
The Netherlands and North Germany
10. c.1510-c.1650 Sweelinck, Cornet, Scheidt, etc.
11. c.1610-c.1700 H. & J. Praetorius, Scheidemann, Tunder, Buxtehude
12. c.1650-c.1710 Weckman, Buxtehude, Bruhns, Böhm
South Germany and Austria
15. c.1660-c.1700 Kerll, Murschhauser, Pachelbel, Muffat, etc.
Italy:
18. 1615-c.1700 Frescobaldi, Rossi, Fasolo, B. Pasquini, etc.

The Progressive Organist (8 vols.)* — Novello/Trevor
(some are for manuals only)
Oortmerssen: A Guide to Duo & Trio Playing* — Boeyenga-Sneek
Organ Book (6 vols.) — OUP/Trevor
Music for Funeral and Remembrance Services — Novello/Trevor
Ceremonial Music for Organ (2 vols.) — OUP
An Easy Album & A Second Easy Album — OUP
Easy Modern Music for Organ (2 vols.) — OUP
Festal Voluntaries (6 vols. linked to the Church Year) — Novello
Organ Music for Services of Thanksgiving — OUP/Trevor
A Second Album of Preludes & Interludes — OUP
Ausgewählte Orgelstücke der Romantik (Vol. 14) — Schott/Busch
Orgelmusik der Klassik und Romantic — Möseler/Stockmeier

Alain: Deux Chorals	Philippo (UMP)	Dupré Le Tombeau de Titelouze (16 Chorales)* 79 Chorales, opus 28* Trois Élevations	Bornemann (UMP) Gray (Belwin Mills) Philippo (UMP)
Alain: 5 pièces faciles	Leduc (UMP)	Eben: Versetti (1 & 2)	Universal
Andriessen: Theme & Variations	Van Rossum, Kalmus	Francaix: Suite Carmelite	Transatlantiques (UMP)
Bach, J. S.: Organ Works* (selected pieces) (some are for manuals only)	Breitkopf/Lohmann Novello Peters Dover	Franck: Organ Works (Selected pieces)	Durand (UMP) Universal
Bairstow: 3 Short Preludes	OUP	Gerber: Four Inventions*	Novello/Jeans
Bohm, G: Organ Works	Breitkopf/Beckmann Kalmus	Guilain: Livre d'Orgue (some are for manuals only)	Schott Kalmus
Brahms: Organ Works	Breitkopf 6062	Hanff: Chorale Preludes	Breitkopf/Beckmann
Bridge: 1st Book of Organ Pieces	Boosey & Hawkes	Hasse N: Sämtliche Orgelwerke	Breitkopf
Britten: Prelude & Fugue on a theme of Vittoria	Boosey & Hawkes	Heiller, A: Nun komm', der Heiden Heiland (variations)	Doblinger 02375**
Bruhns: Organ Works	Breitkopf 6670	Hesse A.: 12 studies with pedal obbligato	Novello
Buxtehude: Organ Works	Breitkopf/Lohmann Hansen-Chester/Hedar	Hindemith: 3 Sonatas (selected movements)	Schott
Darke: Meditation on Brother James' Air	OUP	Hollins: A Trumpet Minuet	Novello
Davies: Interlude in C	Basil Ramsey	Hovland: Orgelkoraler, Vols. 4, 5 & 6	Chester
deGrigny: Livre d'orgue (selected movements)	le Pupitre 68 (UMP) Kalmus	Howells: Psalm Preludes (2 sets)	Novello
Dubois: Toccata in G	Leduc (UMP)	Hurford: 5 Short Chorale Preludes	OUP
duMage: Livre d'orgue (some are for manuals only)	Schott Kalmus		

**This set of variations was originally intended as a model for improvisation, and m[...]
be studied as such by an advanced student.

Ireland:	
Complete Organ Works	Novello
Jacques M.:	
Pavane, Alman & Galliard	Basil Ramsey
Jongen:	
Petit Prélude	OUP
Karg-Elert	
Chorale improvisations from opus 65 (2 vols.)	British & Continental
Kauffmann:	
Harmonische Seelenlust (Preludes on German Chorales)* (some have pedals)	Breitkopf
Kellner:	
Preludes, Trios (Incognita Organo 18)*	Harmonia
Kittel:	
3 Preludes	Novello/Emery
Knecht:	
3 Fugues	Doblinger
Krebs (L) & Stötzel:	
Trios (Incognita Organo 2)*	Harmonia
Langlais:	
Organ Book (10 pieces)	Elkin Vogel
3 Characteristic Pieces	Novello
Mors et Resurrectio	Philippo (UMP)
Lefébure-Wély:	
Sortie in Bb	Harmonia
Leighton:	
6 Fantasies on Hymn-tunes	Basil Ramsey
Lindberg:	
Gammal Fabodpsalm	Chester
Lübeck:	
Organ Works (selected pieces)	Breitkopf/Beckmann
Mendelssohn:	
6 Sonatas (selected movements)	Novello, Breitkopf or Henle
Merkel:	
9 Short Pieces, opus 15	Novello
12 Preludes, opus 156	Novello
10 Preludes, opus 170	Novello

Messiaen:	
Le Banquet Celeste	Leduc (UMP)
Apparition de l'Église Éternelle	Lemoine (UMP)
Murrill:	
Carillon	OUP
Oley:	
Chorale Preludes (2 vols.)*	Novello
Pachelbel:	
Chaconnes (Incognita Organo 31)	Harmonia
Peeters:	
Hymn-Preludes for the Liturgical Year, opus 100* (over 200 pieces in 24 vols.)	Peters
Aria	Heuwekemeijer (Peters)
Reger:	
Choral-vorspiele, opus 67	Breitkopf
Choral-vorspiele, opus 135a	Peters
Rembt:	
6 Trios for Organ	Schott/Jeans
Rheinberger:	
15 selected trios from opus 49 & 189	Novello
12 Monologues, opus 162	Novello
Rinck:	
12 Trios (Incognita Organo 15)*	Harmonia
Scheidemann:	
15 Praeludien und Fugen	Kistner u. Siegel
Schroeder:	
Sechs Orgelchoräle	Schott
Self A.:	
5 Short Pieces	Novello
Sjögren:	
12 Legends (2 vols.)	Chester
Sorge:	
11 Orgeltrios (Incognita Organo 8)*	Harmonia
Stanford:	
Short Preludes & Postludes (2 sets)	Stainer & Bell
Steel:	
6 Pieces for organ	Novello
Suite: Changing Moods	Basil Ramsey

Sumsion:	
Air, Berceuse & Procession	Novello
Thalben-Ball:	
Elegy	Paxton
Thiman:	
8 Interludes (sets 1-3)	Novello
Tunder:	
Vier (4) Praeludien	Kistner u. Siegel
Vaughan Williams:	
Rhosymedre	Stainer & Bell
Vierling:	
5 Trios (Incognita Organo 26)*	Harmonia
Vierne:	
24 Pièces en style libre (2 vols.)	Durand (UMP)
(selected pieces)	
Walther:	
Organ Works (3 Vols.)	Breitkopf/Lohmann
Walton:	
3 Pieces	OUP
Weckman:	
Organ Works	Bärenreiter
Whitlock:	
5 Short Pieces	OUP
Plymouth Suite	OUP
4 Extemporizations	OUP
Willan:	
6 Chorale Prleudes	OUP

BIBLIOGRAPHY

David & Mendel (eds.), *The Bach Reader (A life of J. S. Bach in Letters and Documents),* The Norton Library

Walter Emery, *Notes on Bach's Organ Works,* Novello

John Butt, *Bach Interpretation (Articulation Marks in Primary Sources of J. S. Bach),* Cambridge University Press

Peter Williams, *The Organ Music of J. S. Bach,* 3 Volumes, Cambridge University Press

Quentin Faulkner, *J. S. Bach's Keyboard Technique: An Historical Introduction,* Concordia Publishing House

Stauffer and May (eds.), *J. S. Bach as Organist,* Batsford

Thomas Harmon, *The Registration of J. S. Bach's Organ Works,* Uitgeve Frits Knuf B.V.

Kerala J. Snyder, *Dietrich Buxtehude (Organist in Lübeck),* Schirmer Book a Division of Macmillan, Inc., New York

Arnold Dolmetsch, *The Interpretation of Music of the 17th & 18 centuries,* Repr., Washington University Press

Thurston Dart, *The Interpretation of Music,* Hutchinson University Libra London

Robert Donington, *The Interpretation of Early Music,* Faber & Faber

John Caldwell, *English Keyboard Music Before the 19th Centu* Blackwell, Oxford

Sandra Soderlund, *Organ Technique: An Historical Approach,* Hinsha Music

Tercentenary Essays, Bach, Handel, Scarlatti, Cambridge University Pre

Frederick Neumann, *Ornamentation in Baroque and Post-Baroque Mus* Princeton University Press

Robert Donington, *Baroque Music (Style & Performance – A Handboo* Faber & Faber

Fenner Douglass, *The Language of the Classical French Organ,* Ya University Press

Howard Ferguson, *Keyboard Interpretation,* Oxford University Press

Peter le Huray, *Authenticity in Performance (18th century case studie* Cambridge University Press

Rollin Smith, *Toward an Authentic Interpretation of the Organ Works César Franck,* (Juilliard Performance Guide – 1), Pendragon Press

British Institute of Organ Studies Journals, Positif Press

Andrew Freeman and John Rowntree, *Father Smith,* Positif Press

Clutton and Niland, *The British Organ,* Batsford

William Leslie Sumner, *The Organ,* MacDonald

Peter Williams, *The European Organ (1450-1850),* Batsford

Herbert and H. John Norman, *The Organ Today,* David & Charles

Peter Williams & Barbara Owen, *The Organ* (New Grove Musi Instrument Series), Macmillan

Peter Williams, *A New History of the Organ,* Faber & Faber

Arthur Wills, *Organ,* Yehudi Menuhin Music Guide, Macdonald. (T contains two useful chapters on improvisation, which will take t student further than this tutor)

Peter Hurford, *Making Music on the Organ,* Oxford

11 Glossary

ACCESSORIES   This term is applied to all types of playing aids, such as swell pedals, thumb pistons, toe pistons and composition pedals, except for the speaking stops, manuals and pedalboard.

ACTION   The means by which pipes are sounded by depressing the keys, e.g. mechanical (tracker) action, pneumatic action, electric action.

BAROQUE   This term is used to describe the music of the period from about 1600-1750. The Baroque organ is usually the term applied to the organs of Bach's lifetime. A Neo-Baroque organ is an instrument influenced by the recent revival of interest in organs of the Bach era.

BELLOWS   The apparatus designed to hold wind in readiness to feed the soundboards (and consequently the pipes) which the organist wishes to use.

BLOWER   An electrically operated machine which supplies the bellows or reservoir with wind.

BROKEN OCTAVE   see SHORT OCTAVE.

CASE, CASEWORK   The name for the front (often highly ornate) and side housing of an organ. The front aspect usually includes a display of pipes (often with the occasional dummy to enhance the visual impression), and the sides are often panelled. The study of organ cases is rewarding and inspiring. Frequently the organ case is the most beautiful piece of furniture in a cathedral or church.

CHAMBER ORGAN   A small organ suited to a room, or for continuo work.

CHEST   Another term for the 'wind-chest', or 'soundboard' on which the pipes stand.

CHAIR(E) ORGAN   see POSITIVE.

CHOIR   This is often the name of the lowest manual in an organ with three or more manuals. It comprises a number of quiet stops and is often enclosed in its own expression box. This department is not the equivalent of the Positive organ of the German and French schools of organ-building (see POSITIVE).

CHORUS   A group of stops of the same sonority or family containing one stop at each pitch, forming an integrated ensemble (e.g. the Diapason chorus). The chorus reeds are those suitable for use with the Diapasons, as opposed to Solo reeds, such as Tuba or Fanfare Trumpet.

CIPHER   A fault which causes a pipe or pipes to sound without a key being depressed.

COMBINATION or COMPOSITION PEDALS   Usually to be found on mechanical or pneumatic action organs. Operated by the feet, they appear as metal levers above the pedalboard and assist in changing the stops whilst both hands are occupied.

CONSOLE   The place from which the organist plays his instrument, comprising keyboard(s), pedalboard (where there is one), stops and accessories.

COMPOUND STOPS   Those with more than one pipe to each key.

CORNET   Usually a chorus of open or stopped, wide-scaled Flutes, combined to be activated by one stop-knob, comprising the following pitches: 8′, 4′, 2⅔′, 2′, 1⅗′. The *Cornet séparé* refers to such a chorus in the French organ, which has its own separate chest, as opposed to the *Cornet décomposé* which is made up of stops at the appropriate pitches on either the Grand Orgue or Positif.

COUPLER   The term applied to the accessories which enable the different keyboards to be coupled to each other. These usually take the form of normal draw or tab stops, but occasionally they are to be found as hitch-down pedals.

CRESCENDO PEDAL   A foot-operated pedal, similar to a swell-pedal, which is designed to add stops or subtract them gradually in order to achieve a crescendo or diminuendo using the whole instrument (i.e. all departments coupled). The stopknobs are not activated by this device.

DIAPASON   see OPEN DIAPASON.

EQUAL TEMPERAMENT   see TEMPERAMENT.

EXTENSION   A term given to the system of organ-building which allows stops of the same character to share pipes; e.g. a 4′ Principal may be extended from an Open Diapason 8′ by means of electric switching (the equivalent of adding an octave coupler). The system can be stretched to include a whole chorus (16′, 8′, 4′, 2⅔′, 2′, Mixtures) all taken from one long rank of pipes. The drawback is that missing notes occur in chords and octaves. This rather unsatisfactory, yet cheap system is fast dying out, with the resurgence of mechanical/tracker action organs.

FLUE   The term given to any kind of pipe which does not contain a reed to help in producing its tone.

FLUTE   The name given to the family of stops producing a broadly similar sound to the orchestral or solo instrumental flute.

FREE COMBINATIONS   A German system of registration aids in which each stop is given up to five small drawknobs (usually colour coded), giving five complete registration systems, any one of which being brought into play at the pressing of a piston. The advantage over the capture system (see chapter 7, p.184) is that the combinations may be adjusted during a performance.

GREAT   The name given to the department containing the main chorus-work in the instrument, all other departments being subsidiary to it.

GREAT AND PEDAL COMBINATIONS COUPLED   The inscription on the stop which combines both Great and Pedal Pistons in order to give a balancing pedal combination to whatever stops are required on the Great organ.

HARMONIC FLUTE 4 ft.   These pipes in harmonic ranks have the bellies of their treble pipes bored with a small hole and are overblown. This has the effect of making a more full sound. The pipes may be up to twice their normal speaking length in the treble. Other stops treated similarly are the Harmonic Trumpet 8' (Trompette Harmonique, Fr.) and Harmonic Piccolo 2'.

KEY   The name given to the balanced lever which is depressed by finger or foot in order to emit wind into a pipe. It is also the term describing the tonal centre of a piece of music.

MANUAL(S)   The keyboard(s) played by the hands.

MECHANICAL ACTION or TRACKER ACTION   The complex system of rods and levers linking the stops and keyboards with the pallets directly beneath the pipes. In a fully mechanical organ it is often only the blower which makes use of electricity.

MIXTURE   The general term for the stop(s) containing two or more ranks of pipes per note (i.e. compound stops), their general function being to reinforce some of the upper partials of the harmonic series adding brightness and often brilliance to the ensemble (see Introduction, p.8).

MONTRE   The French equivalent to the British Open Diapason.

MUTATION   A term usually referring to those stops such as Nazard, Twelfth, Tierce or Larigot which are sounding at an interval other than the unison or its octaves.

OPEN DIAPASON   The fundamental organ tone in the British organ equivalent to the Prinzipal in the German organ and the Montre in the French. The bass pipes often form the front display in the case. The 4' stop in the British organ from the same family is called Principal, but the Prinzipal of the German organ is either 32', 16' or 8' pitch.

ORGANO PLENO   A term used to imply Full Organ. It does not, however, necessarily mean using every stop. A lively Diapason Chorus of 8', 4' and 2' pitches can give the effect of a full sound in a small church. In German Baroque music the complete Prinzipal choruses may be drawn on the Hauptwerk (Gt.) and Positiv with the Prinzipals and Reeds of the Pedal (see Chapter 4, p.136).

PALLET   The valve which allows wind into the pipe(s) pertaining to a given key.

PEDALBOARD   (Pedals). The keyboard played by the feet.

PISTON(S)   **Thumb** pistons are operated by the thumb or fingers and are usually placed under the keys of each manual division to which they pertain. **Toe** pistons are placed just above the pedalboard. Their function is to enable the organist to change stops whilst playing. Sometimes these are adjustable by means of a setter-board or with the aid of a computer memory, thus enabling the organist to set up his own desired combinations to suit the work being performed (see Chapter 7, p.183).

PORTATIVE ORGAN   A very small and ancient instrument with just a few keys, which was carried around in the hands or suspended from the neck whilst being played.

POSITIVE (Eng.), POSITIF (Fr.) POSITIV (Germ.).   The name given to the second most important manual divison to the Great manual. It takes differing forms depending on the context and period in which it was built. For example, in the German Baroque and the French Classical organs it will often be found behind the player's back (Rück Positiv/Positif à dos) but in the Early British organ the equivalent department was called the Chaire organ.

PRINCIPAL, PRINZIPAL (Germ.)   see OPEN DIAPASON.

PULL-DOWNS   The term usually associated with a pedal keyboard which is normal in every sense except that it does not have any pipes of its own. It is coupled permanently to the main manual department.

RANK   A complete row of pipes.

RAVALEMENT   Found in some Classical French organs, the term usually refers to the extension of the Pedal reeds stops downwards to heighten the effect of the bass.

REED   Referring to the brass tongue found in stops of the Trumpet, Oboe, Clarinet. 'The Reeds' normally implies all those ranks whose tone is produced by means of a reed, as opposed to the Flues in which no reeds are employed.

REGISTRANT   An assistant employed to change stops during the course of a movement.

REGISTRATION   The term used for the art of selecting, manipulating and combining stops (or 'Registers') appropriate to the music being performed.

RESERVOIR   Like the bellows, it is a receiver and storer of wind, whose pressure is kept constant by means of springs and/or weights.

ROLLSCHWELLER (WALZE)   A romantic German registration aid, taking the form of a cylindrical device for the feet, which, when activated, causes a *crescendo* or *diminuendo* through the whole organ, without the stopknobs being affected. There is usually a dial on the console within easy sight of the organist, to inform him of the position of the cylinder.

SHORT OCTAVE   From the 16th to the early 19th century, the lowest few notes of the keyboard were often arranged so that only the most common bass notes sounded, possibly to save space and reduce cost. There were differing arrangements of these keys. Here is a common form:

G and AA refer to the G and A below the range of today's keyboard. The BROKEN OCTAVE is an extension of the above idea in which the sharp keys

are divided (front and back), with the back end slightly raised to allow more chromatic notes to be used.

SOLO   Normally the top keyboard in a four-manual organ containing a variety of solo stops, such as Tuba (a very loud reed stop often capable of soloing out in single notes above the full organ), Clarinet and Orchestral Oboe.

SOUNDBOARD   The chest on which the pipework stands.

SPECIFICATION   The details of the design of an organ. This may mean simply the list of stops and accessories available in a particular instrument, or it can include all sorts of details such as pipe measurements, case design, materials, and positioning of the instrument, such as an Organ-builder or Consultant might draw up when planning a new organ.

STOP   (Drawstop, stop-knob, register, tab-stop, stop-key). This is the means by which a rank of pipes is brought into play. It can also refer to the rank of pipes associated with a stop.

STRING   The name given to the family of stops producing a broadly similar sound to the orchestral or solo stringed instruments.

SUB-OCTAVE   A coupler which automatically causes all notes played on the manual concerned to play one octave below in addition. Usually found in the Swell organ.

SUPER-OCTAVE   A coupler which automatically causes all notes played on the manual concerned to play one octave above in addition. Usually found in the Swell organ.

SWELL   Normally the upper keyboard in a two or three-manual organ. Its pipes are enclosed in a box (swell-box), one side of which has openable shutters of the Venetian blind variety. These are controlled by a pedal (the swell-pedal) which causes them to open or close, thus causing a *crescendo* or *diminuendo*. There are basically two different kinds of swell-pedal: the 'balanced' one in which the pedal is placed centrally above the pedal-board; and the 'ratchet' pedal, (a lever operated by the right foot), which is situated to the right of the pedalboard.

TEMPERAMENT   A general term referring to tuning. **Equal Temperament** is the one usually used in modern organs, in which the octave is divided relatively equally, enabling performance in any key. **Mean-Tone** tuning favoured certain common keys, and other varieties of temperament have special qualities which add character to the key, and allow greater or lesser chromaticism. Many tunings other than Equal Temperament may become unpleasant to the ear in keys with more than three flats or sharps. There is currently a revival of different temperaments in order to present old music in the way in which it would have been heard at the time of composition.

TRACKER ACTION.   See MECHANICAL ACTION.

TRANSMISSION   A general term for the Action of the organ. It can also denote 'borrowing' in a mechanical organ, e.g. when an 8' Principal is required for a Pedal organ and cost prohibits this, the Open Diapason 8' of the Great may be made playable on the Pedals 'by transmission'.

TRANSPOSITION   The art of raising or lowering the pitch of a piece of music, usually necessary to suit particular voices or congregations (see Chapter 6, p.181).

TREMULANT   A stop which, when drawn causes the wind supply to the soundboard to vibrate, thus causing the sound to undulate. If used carefully and sparingly its effect can be most expressive.

UNISON OFF   This stop is normally used in conjunction with one or other, or both of the octave couplers (see SUB-OCTAVE and SUPER-OCTAVE). It enables all sorts of special colours, especially with the soft registers.

UPPERWORK   A broad term normally meaning stops above 4' pitch.

VENTIL   A valve designed to bring on or to shut off the wind supply to a stop or group of stops, usually by means of a toe pedal. Ventils were used as the most common aid to registration in French Romantic music (see Chapter 7, p.192).

VOICING   One of the many arts of the Organ-builder. Once pipes are made, they have to be made to 'speak' to their best advantage in the organ in which they are to play their part. The voicing of a large organ may take months of careful adjustment.

WALZE   see ROLLSCHWELLER.

WERK PRINZIP   See Chapter 4, p.118 for an explanation.

WIND-CHEST   Another name for SOUNDBOARD.

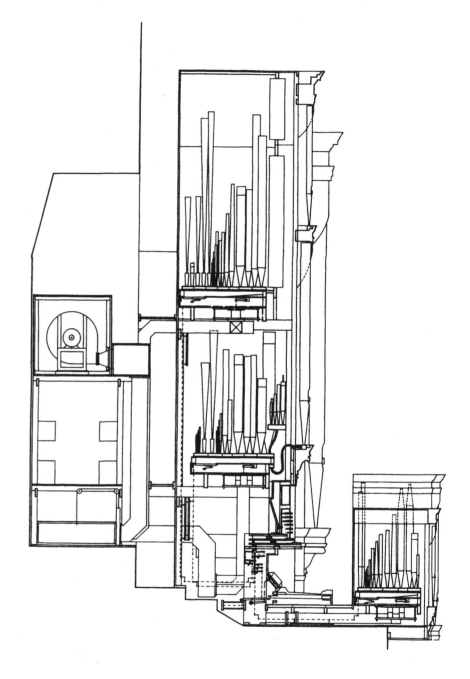

the layout of a traditional organ

Printed and bound in Great Britain by
Caligraving Limited Thetford Norfolk

08/16 (197781)